Praise for *Light of the Infinite*

"Whether you're newly curious about Jewish texts or a seasoned talmudist, *Light of the Infinite* will surprise and delight you. Drawing on a broad range of Jewish sources, Safar weaves seamless lessons of life, love, joy and transcendence. Highly recommended!"
—Accidental Talmudist

"While our culture often exacerbates feelings of inadequacy, stress, competition, and isolation, Erez Safar's *Light of the Infinite* offers a welcome illumination of philosophies and practices that calm inner turmoil and cultivate positivity. We are all seeking joy and harmony inside and outside ourselves... this book provides valuable tools to advance that quest."
—Shepard Fairey, *Obey Giant*

"The authentic spiritual searcher of today won't compromise on anything less than drinking from a fountain of authenticity. This is precisely what one can find when delving into the treasure of teachings of my dear friend, Erez Safar, who has beautifully provided the manuscript in front of you."
—Rav Shlomo Katz

"As author Erez Safar points out, 'Becoming the hero of our own story' is the essence of Jewish learning. *Light of the Infinite* is a wonderful new resource for the study of the profound ideas of Judaism. The book is written with passion, depth, and most importantly—joy."
—Stephen Tobolowsky, actor and author of *My Adventures with God*

"Our journey is one of perpetual desire to simultaneously be present and to transcend, to know and be known, to love and be loved. *Light of the Infinite* joins a chorus of light, illumining the way, guiding us on that journey."
—Zevi Slavin, *Seekers of Unity*

"These pages are filled with love for G-d, Torah and the Jewish people."
—David Sacks, writer and producer of *The Simpsons*

"I am grateful to use these texts to help resynchronize my brain and soul to better enjoy my time on this planet. Fortunate are we for this work that brings the light of our ancestors into the palms of our hand and fortunate are these writings to be added to the blockchain of Israelite wisdom."
—Rabbi Harry Rozenberg, *Trippy*

"With the healing words of The Arizal, Rebbe Nachman, The Alter Rebbe and others in hand, Erez Safar leads us down the circuitous path of being human, vulnerably laying out the vicissitudes of life. But any descent is for the sake of a subsequent ascent into the depths of the Infinite light that saturates the very issues we encounter along Safar's textual path. The reader will always come away feeling lighter, breathing calmer, and just a little bit more hopeful."
—Rav Joey Rosenfeld

"Erez does an elegant job of distilling and synthesizing scripture and commentary, particularly the gematria and the Kabbalistic wisdom, in a deeply accessible way. Reading these pieces every day will enrich anyone's life, and profoundly increase one's Jewish knowledge."
—Adam Mansbach, author of *Go the F**k to Sleep*

"Safar takes you along on an incredibly hopeful journey, tying in music, culture, kabbalah, and scripture, transforming what can sometimes be hard to understand or connect to into something fun and relatable. He turned his pain from recent loss to hope, light, strength, and beauty, encouraging this journey through his faith in a non-judgmental and gentle way. In my personal experience, tough times did not always lead me to connect more, but rather to question more. Safar's writing has helped guide my own growth and connection to spirituality and enabled me to trust all things in life on a deeper level."
—Colleen Davidoff PsyD, LCSW

"Erez told me that one of my lyrics in particular really resonated with him, it's from my song, Lifted and goes, "when confusion takes a hold of me, then I forget who I am, but I don't forget whose I am." This Light of the Infinite book series is a guide to understanding the truth of this statement, highlighting our own inner healing through the spiritual work of unifying with our Creator, never forgetting that we are His and He is ours."
—Nissim Black

"Erez's extraordinary dedication to the weekly Torah portions and the profound chassidic teachings that surround it bring a cool hipster vibe and relevance to anyone seeking light and love in their lives. He's done an astounding job of a magnanimous caliber in this *Light of the Infinite* book series. Erez rocks, his teachings follow suit. He's always surrounded by tremendous light, epic people, and deep teachings.

The fact that Erez has spent countless hours, every week over the course of nearly 2 years, producing these 5 manuscripts as a dedication to his mother's memory, shows that he is a living example of the Torah. A person who takes a tragedy and turns it into a blessing is someone who practices what he preaches.

We have an idea in Judaism that the source of the content has an influence over the content, and the source of this content is not only stimulating intellectual relevant modern hip ideas that connect us to modern culture and Torah, but it also comes from a pure place from a person with such tremendous intentions to raise his mother's soul. Highly recommend this to anyone interested in spirituality and mental health."
—Nili Salem

"In my 2.5 years of learning Daf Yomi, I've generally focused on the Pshat—a literal or direct reading of the text of the Talmud. Occasionally the Remez, the allegorical or symbolic level of learning. But I rarely venture into the Sod. I do not actively seek for the secret meaning, the mystical meaning, the Kabbalistic interpretation, for inspiration.

Light of the Infinite reminds me how important it is to explore these further reaches of understanding regardless of whether I do or do not, at this moment in time, feel a connection to HaShem, or to my spiritual self. All of these aspects together can offer a far greater holistic understanding of the magnificent interlocking facets of Judaism, and the scope of Jewish thought, and Jewish spiritual practice, than what I can gain from only the literal text on the page.

What Erez Safar is doing with *Light of the Infinite* and his dvars is offering an access point to that very feeling of discovery and understanding, in a relatable and illuminating approach. I especially appreciate how Erez juxtaposes quotes from Talmudic sages, Chassidic Rebbes, and noted modern thinkers and leaders with the voices of activists, musicians, and artists—a beautiful merger of art and soul. I think his approach is one that many Jews are looking for, and will connect to in a deep and meaningful way."
— Miriam Anzovin, Daf Reactions

Light of the Infinite
The Sound of Illumination

Erez Safar

Yeh Publishing
an imprint of Bancs, LLC
Los Angeles

ISBN (paperback): 979-8-9867298-9-3
ISBN (hardcover): 979-8-9867298-8-6
ISBN (ebook): 978-1-960281-00-5
ISBN (audiobook): 978-1-960281-01-2

Yeh Publishing, an imprint of Bancs LLC
1976 S. La Cienega Blvd, # 199
Los Angeles, CA 90034
www.yehpub.com

© 2023, Yeh Publishing,
an imprint of Bancs, LLC

www.erezsafar.com
www.lightofinfinite.com

Also by Erez Safar
The Genesis of Light
The Exodus of Darkness

COMING SOON
Transformation in the Desert of Darkness
Emanations of Illumination

Manuscript edits by Ariel Hendelman and Jamie Weissman
Cover design by Armando Marin, Erez Safar and Kleshaam Shakir
Graphic designs by Erez Safar
Illustration of my mother (Frida Levona bat Shalom),
my kids' bubby (Yehudis Chava bat Yakov) and me by Elke Reva Sudin
Book design by Maggie McLaughlin

Printed in the United States

Special Thanks

First off, I have to thank Hashem for bringing me into this world and honoring me with an opportunity to shine some of the Infinite Light into this finite physicality. I have to thank my parents as partners with Hashem in bringing me into this world and inspiring me in so many different ways, both creatively and intellectually. Especially my mom, who helped me become humble, while at the same time showing me that I can do anything my heart desires. She was the biggest supporter and inspiration in my life. I still mourn her passing every moment and pray for a speedy reunification with the building of the Third Temple. In the meantime, I have devoted my work to her and her *Aliyat Neshama*, and I am so thankful for having my sister in my life, with whom I can navigate this space and life. I have to thank my kids (Dovi and Moshi) for inspiring me every moment. I have never known a love like this and all the time I spend with them is the biggest and brightest gift I have ever experienced.

We can see how fast life moves when we look at children, more so other people's children who we see less often, when we see how much they have grown. It's why it is so important to be present in every moment to the fullest extent; to fully live. In *Parashah* Mishpatim, we read that Hashem says to Moshe, *Come up to the mountain and be there* (וַיֹּאמֶר ה' אֶל־מֹשֶׁה עֲלֵה אֵלַי הָהָרָה וֶהְיֵה־שָׁם).[1] Rabbi Shlomo Carlebach points out that most of the time we are not where we are; we are somewhere else. Even with Moshe Rabbainu, even on his level, being invited to come to the mountain for 40 days, even in that instance, Hashem feels the need to say, "*Ve'h'yeh sham*," to make sure Moshe is spiritually present while being physically present. The lesson is that when we are in a space of knowing how much we don't know, when we are in a state of *bitul* (self-nullification), not in a space of thinking we know this

vii

and we know that, but that we don't really know anything, in the space of *nishmah*, that is being fully present; of being deeper in the space spiritually, just as much as physically. That is where true growth happens.

The Ishbitzer Rebbe asks what the purest thing in the world is and answers his own question saying, "life itself!" There is nothing holier, purer, deeper that flows down from Hashem than life itself. The question that each of us must answer is how much life do we receive and what do we do with it? So when Hashem is saying to Moshe to be truly *there*, He is saying, "You have to go through life and be present for life to go through you, and so to be truly there is to be truly alive, to be fully present, to be in the space of *nishmah*."

Carlebach reminds us that we are not really living yet: "We are only half alive. How could it be that one minute we are good, one minute we are bad? One minute we are holy, one minute we are unholy? One minute we love, one minute we hate?" He explains that we never have a place of our own or stand firmly in place. We jump around from one place to another, not gaining anything from the experience. Hashem is telling Moshe (and us) that we have to reach for the level on which life itself can flow purely into us.[2] It is my intention in writing this book to help myself achieve this level, as well as everyone who reads this.

I would like to thank Jamie Weissmann, who has edited these Divrei Torah every week since I started this project, and Ariel Hendelman for doing the final edits on the manuscript. Finally, I would also like to thank everyone who has supported the Light of Infinite project!

Contents

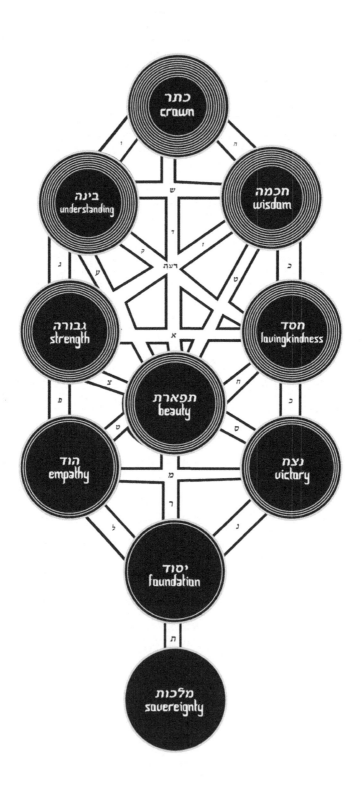

Prologue

In this Light of the Infinite book series, I act as your spiritual DJ, curating mystical insights into the weekly Torah portion and the infinite light of Kabbalah. Just like on the dance floor, where the right song at the right moment can elevate your physical being, it's my hope that this book will elevate your spiritual being in the moments when you need it most.

This weekly Torah project and book series began on the *Yartzeit* (yearly memorial) of my ex wife's mother's passing, and it's inspired by both her (*Yehudis Chava bat Yakov Dov*) and my mother (*Frida Levona bat Shalom*), who passed the same year. When I think of these women, I think of *tzedakah* and *chesed*, words that are hard to translate because they capture the real depths of other adjectives like 'generous', 'giving', 'loving', and 'kind'. These two women embodied and exemplified these qualities to an angelic degree: so full of life, love, warmth, and light, at every turn, every single moment. Being around them inspired me to be more loving, more giving, more full of zest for each moment in life.

My goal with this project is to spread that inspiration and Light that I received, and still receive, from them. Using each week's Torah portion, delving deep into the text, the commentaries, and the Kabbalah connected to it, I'll share insights that bring that inspiration and Light to life for me, and hopefully do the same for you.

As DJ Shadow sampled on his seminal record, *Entroducing,* "It's not me that's coming through—the music's coming through me." With that said, I do not take any recognition for any part of the material except the writing style. The recognition is meant for the Holy One, Blessed be He, and the Giants of Torah that reveal the

1

Light of Infinite in a way that only they can. So, I would like to give thanks to some of the Chassidic Masters and Rabbis that I draw the most inspiration from, whose wisdom I'm attempting to bring down and make accessible. Please see the section on Rabbinic sources for more information on all of the Chassidic masters and Rabbis whose wellsprings I drew from for this book.

I hope that these words inspire you to delve deeper into the Torah and kabbalistic texts, and, as Chaim Vital says, "One can go deeper and deeper, as far as the human mind can delve, and it will always yield new treasures."

WHERE THE JOURNEY STARTED

There are moments in each of our lives that we can recognize as turning points, moments in which we resonate with something in a way that we never have previously. I remember when I read Oscar Wilde and Dostoyevsky, I never again looked at books as something associated with school or boredom; instead I looked at them with reverence and curiosity. A new hunger was awakened, a new wonder if I would be able to write in a way that would satiate someone else's longing for literature. I knew that I'd never read in the same way, and I'd only ever write with passion, with a weighted pen and with not only myself in mind, but in the hopes to ignite a passion in anyone reading my musings.

I've always been drawn to Kabbalah, starting with devouring anything by Aryeh Kaplan, intrigued by the esoteric secrets of the eventual perfection intended to come out of the chaos of creation. How could that not capture every ounce of my interest? To an outsider, Judaism can seem a heavy religion of obligation and guilt. I would venture to say some of that did seep into the tradition through the culture of Christianity, as so many Jews were exiled in Eastern Europe. But Chassidism, especially through Chabad and Breslov, brings us back to our roots, while skyrocketing us to the future redemption—all through shifting obligation to honor and guilt to gratitude.

My dad was a Rabbi in the Navy, so we moved every few years throughout my childhood. It allowed me to live far outside the box and experience life and society in new ways fairly often. Beginning in college, I gravitated toward Chabad because of their acceptance of every living soul, recognizing that we all are children of God, and just as we are guests in God's house (this world), so too are we treated as such in the Chabad houses around the world. There was a warmth and a love there both for the tradition and the Book, as well as the People of the Book and the people who have not yet found it.

What I didn't know was that while I always felt part Chabad, the other part of me was very much Breslov. In 2008, I was performing in Yalta, the Black Sea in Ukraine. I stayed in Kiev for Shabbat and being so close to Uman, the site where Rebbe Nachman is buried and so many of his followers flock to every Rosh Hashanah, I couldn't miss the chance to jump into a cab and make my way there. It was a month after Rosh Hashanah, and there was only one soul that I could spot—the groundskeeper, along with his dog. I made my way to the *kever* (grave) and said *Tikkun Haklali* (Rebbe Nachman's compilation of *tehilim* for complete fixing/ healing). On the way back, I put my headphones on and listened to Erez Yechiel singing the Tikkun in his Yemenite style, and I felt on fire for Hashem, my soul connected on a deep level, in the presence of one of the Chassidic masters, a link in an unbroken chain to the Source.

I started to study *Likutei Moharan* on my own every Shabbat. But it wasn't until I met David Ben Yehuda ten years later, one year for each sphere and *sefira*, that I fully comprehended how Breslov I really am. The way that Breslov views the Torah not as narrative stories of our mothers and fathers or of laws, but of us—our stories we live every day, our nature that we struggle within and strive to reach beyond. In the text, Esav and Yakov battle, so we learn from it in whatever way we can. But the real story is that we each have an Esav and Yakov within us, and the battle is actually in our lives every day. It's our own Yakov that must subdue and elevate our own Esav. It's our own Egypt and enslavements that we must escape; overcoming ourselves, reaching our own redemptions. Amalek isn't just a nation we are commanded to rid from the earth, but a notion we must illuminate from our very being. Amalek has the same gematria (numerical value) as *Safek*, which means doubt—it's the crippling effects of doubt that we must remove from ourselves, so we can be fully free.

Having spent my formative years in Hebrew Academy of Greater Washington, Yeshiva of Greater Washington, Tiferet Yerushalayim, Bayit VeGan, and Ohr Sameach in Ma'alot Dafna, I now spend my time with my two sons, Dovi and Moshi, producing music and visuals, writing, and in and out of *chavruta* with David Ben Yehudah studying the texts of Rebbe Nachman, Reb Natan, The Alter Rebbe and The Lubavitcher Rebbe.

About the Author

Based out of the stereophonic heart of Los Angeles, Erez Safar, award-winning producer, is a creative machine and gallerist. Safar is also the Founder/CEO of Bancs Media, a celebrated production and marketing company; Slay Sonics, a powerhouse indie resource and music marketing platform; The Elemental Life; Guru and You, a telemedicine treatment platform; and Bancs Gallery, a creative art space and art gallery in Los Angeles.

Safar has also just launched a new project, Don't Block Your Blessings, to honor his mom's memory. The goal is to collect and present an online living library of stories, performances, light and love to a world in need of healing. As part of this project, Safar launched a first-of-its-kind live-stream festival featuring musicians, artists, and some of the most innovative minds in self-growth and healing.

The DBYB Festival boasts three interactive rooms on an exclusive virtual platform, allowing festival goers to jump from room to room attending talks and sessions, accessing musical performances, and viewing live art as it is created. The last festival featured cast members from Broadway's Hamilton joining The-Piano-Art-Project. People all over the world have been sharing videos of positivity and perspective as part of it, including Justin Long (*Waiting, Accepted, Dodgeball*), David Sacks (writer of *The Simpsons* and creator of the Spiritual Tools for an Outrageous World podcast), Autumn Reeser (*Entourage, The OC*), Mayim Bialik (*Blossom, Big Bang Theory*), and Wayne Coyne (The Flaming Lips).

Safar was grateful to be recognized as one of the world's most influential Jews in the Forward's annual "Forward 50" list. His companies have graced Billboard magazine, and he has been featured on *NPR*, *The New York Times*, *USA Today*, and *The Wall Street Journal*, among others.

Safar is dedicated to bringing diverse people together through education workshops and public appearances with his artists, while creating safe spaces for dialogue and healing. Safar's eclectic skill set, varied experience, and passion to help others gives him a unique perspective and insight into a broad variety of critical topics that affect us all.

Story About My Children's Grandmothers

For my children, losing their two grandmothers in one year was difficult. They grew up having both a "Savta" and a "Bubbie." They called my mother, Frida Levona bat Shalom, "Savta," because she was Israeli and Yeminite. They called their mother's mother, Yehudis Chava bat Yakov, "Bubbie," because of her Eastern-European descent.

Story about Bubbie

 I wanted to share a bit more about my kids' bubbie (Mrs. Baitz), as she was such an inspiration to me, the living personification of *Chesed* (loving kindness).

I have never met anyone like Mrs. Baitz before, someone so full of life, love and light, at every turn, every single moment. She inspired me to express these same attributes in myself. She had so many blissful moments with her eleven kids and their kids. It's hard to imagine a world without her in it; showering her family with goodness. May her *neshama* (soul) have an *aliyah* (elevation).

Her daughter/my kids' mother (Nina Safar) wrote this, and I just had to share it:

> *"When my mother passed, a piece of my heart went with her. Buried in a place I couldn't reach. A week later, my father ended up in the hospital on a ventilator, fighting Covid for months, and that space was quickly filled with fear. When he returned home, the fear slowly left, but the space was still there, a hollowed heart begging to be filled, only nothing could fill it.*

Inhaling her perfume, reading her texts and staring at photos of her unleashed memories that only hurt more, like paper cuts to the heart. The grief of missing her was a constant reminder of the distance between us and the finality of it.....

What I've noticed these last few months....

.....is that when I'm with my family—my boys...my siblings... and most of all my father—it almost feels like the love that we share for her can somehow fill that space up. Almost. Not completely. But when I am laughing with my siblings, filled with pride over something my boys are doing, or looking at my father resting in our childhood home.....

.......in those moments, if I close my eyes and reach for her, I can feel my mother there with us. Her love. Her warmth. It wraps over me, and in those few moments my broken heart feels full."

Story about Savta

Written 10/27/20: All that we crave and need is love and support in its many manifestations. My mom always gave me that—every song I made, every poem I wrote, every show I played. She and my *Savta* and my entire Yemenite family were the inspiration for both Shemspeed (the label I started back in the day and toured the world with (Berlin, Jerusalem, Kyiv, London, Melbourne, Moscow, Paris, Sydney, Tel Aviv, Yalta, and literally all over the states...) and the big inspiration behind my Sephardic Music Festival, which ran for 12 years in NY and LA over the 8 days of Chanukah every year. Both The NY Times and

The Wall Street Journal covered the festival with two-page spreads and photos—it was incredible. The tens of thousands of people that would come to the sold out events (shows, symposiums, parties, family events) over the years got a little taste of the music and history of the Jews indigenous to the Middle East. Hopefully, they also saw how much shared culture and history we have with all the peoples in that area. So much of division and hate is based on lack of knowledge and history, and a focus on the "Other." My purpose in putting these festivals on, year after year, was to highlight not the "otherness' but the Oneness.

My mom would come up every year for opening or closing night of the festival and get to see sold-out crowds enjoying the sort of music she had me grow up listening to. The two compilations I put out, which you can hear on Spotify, have Matisyahu with Yehuda Solomon singing a Yemenite chorus from the diwan, the legendary songstress Yasmin Levy, Watcha Clan, Yair Dallal, Sarah Aroeste in Ladino being remixed by Tamir of Balkan Beat Box, and so many more incredible artists. All the sorts of music my mom and I love so much.

I was on a flight on the way back East again to see her. Scared I might not arrive in time, I called my friend Idan Raichel to sing and let her know that I was on my way. He did just that, and it showed how much love there was around her. I really just want to thank all the hundreds of musicians that believed in all these projects, because the truth is, it was all born of a dream my mom had. Love y'all!

Written 12/2/20: I felt moved to share something more about my mom, since this project is in her memory.

My mom taught Talmud to women, made sculptures, painted, and played accordion ... I mean, she was an incredible force. I see her in my kids, and I'm thankful for that. Her parents moved to Israel around 1927. She grew up making art and music. She was the oldest and played mother to her younger siblings. In her 20s, my mom worked with special needs kids doing art therapy; her medium was sculpture and illustration. After meeting my dad in Israel, she moved to America and became an *au pair* in Chicago where he lived. They got married and moved to New York where she studied Talmud at JTS, then moved to Miami shortly after to become the Rebbetzin (a term she disliked) at the University of Miami. As my dad enlisted in the U.S. Navy as a Chaplain, they moved to San Diego, Japan, South Carolina, Italy, Illinois, Maryland.

She took courses at the local universities and accumulated enough credits to sit for the CPA exam and went on to rise to the top of her profession. At the time when she took the CPA exam, even though she had only started learning English in her mid twenties, she succeeded in passing all four parts of the CPA exam on her first try—a rarity. She joined various firms and then eventually became a named partner in a public accounting firm in Bethesda, MD. It is rare for anyone to have such a strong hold on both the right and left sides of their brain, but my mom was not just anyone, as everyone who came by to console us in our time of mourning said. What made her so unique was that she was such a strong woman, but at the same time had such a soft and loving side to her, making all that came in contact with her feel warm.

I learned almost everything from my mother by just seeing how she navigated and loved the journey of it all. We connected on so many things, but one of the most special was going to concerts together. Two in particular stand out—one was Buena Vista Social Club and the other was seeing McCoy Tyner at the Blues Alley in D.C. I had him sign the cover of my all-time favorite album, which he was such a big part of with John Coltrane, "A Love Supreme."

A Love Supreme, indeed.

Sometimes poetry and music are the only way to express your feelings, so that you can live in them in a bearable way... I wrote this one night in 2020, as I was slipping into slumber, thinking about my mom and praying for her health. As I wrote each word, I broke down sobbing...

A love untainted
I expected nothing
given everything
nursed into existence
I followed you around the world
every bit of art inspired by
your family
exiled for thousands of years
eyes on the holy land
showed me about
your love in my little hand
I'm crying as I realize
soon I can't reach out
at least not in this world
but the bits you left
I'll pick them all up
till there's nothing left
put it in my art
set it free
now it's you and me
and the person who
sees
feels
knows
... that it's real.

Hitbodedut
/ Meditation

May we all rid ourselves of doubt, release the chains of our own struggles and the parts of our minds that enslave us, and manifest the Promised Land within ourselves. I'll leave you with this blessing, which are the lyrics to Akiva's gorgeous Breslov Niggun, off his album, אל תעזבי ידיים (Al Ta'azvi Yadayim):

Master of the universe, give me the strength that I can illuminate my face towards every being	ריבונו של עולם, תן לי את הכח להאיר פנים לכל אדם
To see the good points in my friends and not what they are lacking	לראות מעלת חברי ולא חסרונם
Give me the eyes to see the great good and kindness you do in the world	תן לי עיניים לראות בטוב ובחסד שנתת בעולם
That I judge myself and others positively	שאדון לכף זכות את עצמי ואת חבריי
And that I'm constantly humble, and lowly in my own eyes.	שאהיה בענווה תמיד שפל בעיניי
I want to thank you, Hashem on all that I have	אני רוצה להודות לך על כל מה שיש
and I also want to thank you for that which is lacking and help me do it without feeling shame	רוצה להודות גם בחסרון בלי להתבייש
And that I should remember that it's always possible to return, and to fix everything anew.	לזכור שתמיד אפשר לחזור ולתקן הכל, להתחדש

Introduction

In the last book, *The Exodus of Darkness* we read the famous saying *Naaseh v'Nishma* which is Shemot 24:7. This translates as "Everything that Hashem has said, we will do and we will listen (obey)."[1]

So when *B'nei Yisrael* said, "We will do and we will hear," we see that both are needed to be fully connected. We can be present, we can *do*, but the second our ego gets in there, we are no longer tapped into the "we will *hear*." We go from the potential of infinity to being constricted into finitude.

It's only in the *nishma* ("we will hear"), the space of being present, the space of *tefillah (prayer)*, the space of *bitul* (nullification) and *dveykut* (attaching oneself to God) that we become infinite; fully connected to the Infinite One.

We are now in between the book of Shemot (Exodus) and Bamidbar (Numbers). The importance of *nishma* (hearing/listening) and *dveykut* brings to mind a beautiful and deep teaching by Rebbe Nachman and the word *shetikah* (being silent). Rabbeinu teaches that in this silence is wisdom, which we learn from the *midbar* (desert). As it says in Bamidbar, "In the desert you will find a present." This is because in the quiet, in being truly present and listening, wisdom comes to a person. If one is always speaking, thinking they know more than those around them, and not listening, this person is driven by ego, and ego is the death of wisdom. We need to nullify ourselves for wisdom to be granted. *Keter* (crown) around *chochmah* (wisdom).

It is in this space of *na'aseh v'nishma* that we are in unconditional obedience and enthusiasm to fulfill our Creator's *mitzvot* (commandments), regardless of if we understand them rationally.

As it's written in the Talmud, Hashem offered the Torah to *B'nei Yisrael* and instead of asking, "What is written there?" they replied, "*Na'aseh v'nishma.*" It may seem odd to agree to something before fully understanding it, and while we must always understand and learn as much as possible, intellectual knowledge of the Divine can't be a precondition of living within the guidelines set forth by our Creator. It is the "we will do" of observing the *mitzvot* that brings us to an appreciation of them and the unification (aka *dveykut*) with the Divine that they facilitate.

It seems that we are all in various states of Divine disconnect. Some might even say we are spiritually sick. We attempt to heal, but it is a long journey that feels impossible at times. When we attempt to heal our physical selves, it is in much the same way of doing and then hearing/seeing/understanding. When a doctor prescribes the medication we need to heal, we take it in good faith; we don't first go to medical school, researching every element of it and only take the medication afterward. If that were the case, we would remain sick, no doubt getting worse and worse. We take it in faith because it benefits our physical selves and isn't contingent on our knowledge of its inner workings. In fact by taking it, we can start to see clearer, feel better, and get a better understanding of how the medicine helped.[2] It is the same with our spiritual selves—the more we are in the space of *na'aseh v'nishma* with the mitzvot, the more elevated our spirit, and by virtue of that, our physical selves, will be.

The *mitzvot* outline action of unification. It's not enough to think, intellectualize or to pledge oneself—action is what shows *dveykut* (attaching oneself to God). Love isn't intellectual, it's a feeling, and one that must be followed by actions or it fades. To pledge love or faith without action is the beginning of a desire for a thing, but it is not a unification with the thing itself.

In this book, which covers the *parshiot* of Vaykira, *Bechukotai* being one of them, it covers the *chukim* (the *mitzvot* that we cannot rationalize or comprehend). We learn that even those we most follow, for in those we can show our full faith, and connect and reap the benefits both in this world and in the next. In Lukkutei Torah, the Alter Rebbe interprets the term *bechukotai* as related to the word *chakikah* which means "engraved." This is meant to teach us that not only are we commanded to keep the *mitzvot*, but we have to labor in the study and learning of Torah until it is engraved within us. We write the letters of the Torah on parchment, and though independent of the parchment, they become united with it. That is the process of continuing the tradition of writing the Torah. Engraving on a deeper level is when the letters are not an independent entity, as they cannot be separated from the object they have been engraved into. The two become one and that is what *bechukotai* is about: it is when we become one with the Torah that is Hashem in this world.

The Zohar teaches that "The Torah and God are totally one."[3] The Alter Rebbe expounds on this, stating that the Torah, which seems to be a glimmer of the Divine, is actually the wisdom and will of God, and so it is completely one with God. It seems counterintuitive for an infinite light to be one with a finite element on earth given for us, but that is what infinite transcendence is.

It is my hope that these insights into the Torah that I humbly present to you, through ancient wisdom and the teachings of being present in the gift of this presence that we are granted every day resonate with you and inspires you to dive deeper into the endless gems and lessons of life itself contained in the Tanach, Talmud, and other sacred texts that continually flow as infinite light.

How to Exist in Love: Tending to the Spirit

Before we dive into the chapters of this book, there are some key teachings/principles that are vital to reaching higher and more expansive states of spirituality and wholeness. I will highlight a few here.

The concept of doing something **Lishmah** (for its sake) is crucial in living in alignment with both oneself and our Source. It's the inner spiritual work when done with the physical performance of *mitzvot* that sanctifies our being. The Zohar stresses that *ahavah* (love) and *yirah* (awe) are the two main ingredients needed for Torah and *mitzvot* to affect their ultimate purpose.

We need to rid ourselves of our self-serving nature by practicing **bitul hayesh** (negating and nullifying traces of ego, of self-centeredness). It is through this that we can align as creations with our Creator. Our focus can manifest our falls, so we need to ensure we are aiming for faith and alignment. With humility and gratitude, a person becomes a partner in creation, as Rebbe Nachman explains, "Hashem created this world because of His mercy, and He created the entire world in order to reveal His mercy."[1]

By believing that everything is ultimately held by a larger Good and returning to a place of gratitude, a person binds themselves to the Creator— fulfilling Hashem's ultimate goal for creating the universe. Hashem's mercy will always prevail over such a person and constantly increase. It's as The Tzemach Tzedek would say, "**Tracht gut, vet zein gut**," which translates as "*Think good and it will be good.*" That must be each person's motto, in realizing that full faith brings ultimate good and redemption. It's the realization that we can't get along without the Infinite One, and that the **bitachon** (trust) in *hashgacha pratit* (Divine providence) brings us closer to the truth of "**Ein od Milvado**"—"There is nothing other than God." It is often the ones furthest from Hashem who are able to find their *bitachon* when they are suffering. They realize that calling out to God is their only option.

The Lubavitcher Rebbe says, "**We have only, by faith, to compensate for those moments of faithlessness.**" I've always seen time as a figment of a fractured world; a perspective limited by finitude. Our limited selves are trapped in a constant struggle: *Amalek* (the nation and notion we are tasked to eliminate) is the manifestation of *safek*, the doubt that grows in places of narrow physicality, while the constant practice of eliminating *safek* is the expansion of ever-broadening spiritual reality. It's only by that expansion and unification with the Divine Truth that each person can tap into the light of the Infinite, our Godly soul, unbound by time.

In our physical reality, it seems that in almost every moment of our lives we are caught between two choices: the easier or more selfish choice and something a bit harder, a selfless choice. Sometimes *safek* (doubt) blurs the lines between the two, but often, if we tap into **emunah** (faith) and our gut, we know which is the one for us. Every action affects every other action. The fact that it takes so long to break a habit shows that every single action has ramifications far beyond it. That's why it says in Pirkei Avot, *The reward for a mitzvah is a mitzvah,*[2] if doing good begets doing good, one can take action to stay in perpetual goodness, or God forbid, struggle steeped in the opposite. Too much *chesed* (loving kindness) without the balancing attribute of *gevurah* (judgment) to reach a state of *tiferet* (harmony) is also not healthy. The struggle between *chesed* and *gevurah* is within us at all times.

The story of **Yakov and Esav** polarizes these two sides, but since one represents the *yetzer tov* (good inclination) and the other the *yetzer hara* (evil inclination), and because both exist within us, it makes it that much tougher to see them clearly. Even with Yitzchak, their father, we see that (in *parashat* Toldot) he wanted to give the blessings to Esav, since when something is so close to you, it's hard to see it clearly.

As we learn in *Chassidut*, **every descent is for the sake of an even greater ascent**. Viewed in this way, there are truly no mistakes, but rather pitfalls that have the potential to become springboards. We see this throughout the timeline of our journey. Adam had six *mitzvot* (commandments), Noah had seven, and then extra *mitzvot* were given to each Patriarch (even though we learn that they kept all of Torah before it was given). But when we fast forward through the initial journey to the giving of the Torah, we see the closeness and chosenness, "and You have chosen us."[3] This is greater than all the moments preceding. The Lubavitcher Rebbe articulates that this was a revelation of Hashem's essence, something that had not occurred prior.

As Isaiah articulates, **"The Glory of the Lord will be revealed."**[4] The level of closeness and revelation of Hashem when Moshiach arrives will be far greater than any revelation experienced previously.

Yakov is referred to as "the choicest of forefathers," implying his service was greater than that of his fathers. In regards to the other holy patriarchs, Avraham and Yitzchak, the Arizal teaches that their ways of relating to and serving the Holy One contained some element of imbalance, which manifested as an imperfection in their offspring. Unrestrained love, which Avraham embodies, can turn into loving the wrong things. Unrestrained awe, which Yitzhak embodies, can turn into awe of the wrong things. We see that although Avraham brought Yitzchak into this world, he also brought Yishmael into the world, and likewise, though Yitzchak brought Yakov into the world, he also had Esav.

Only Yakov's sons were all righteous because the attribute of mercy, which he embodies by virtue of his complete connection to the Torah, is by definition, intelligent emotionality and as such can perfect both love and awe, and is resistant to improper application.[5]

Thus it was that Yakov, who brought B'nei Yisrael into the world, birthed the entire Jewish people with the 12 tribes.

Nevertheless, even decades later, with the revelations at Sinai that brought a transformation to holiness, our world was not yet utterly transformed, as we see so shortly after with the potential to sin played out through the Golden Calf. But in the time of Moshiach, there won't be a temporal Divine altering, but a complete shift from the potential of impurity that manifests as the *sitra achra* (other side) to only one side, the side of *Emet* (truth). Division will be destroyed which will also mean full internal unity and the absence of our divisive impulse towards evil.

Falls bring elevation: the descent to Egypt brings the ascent to the Promised Land, and so it is in our own lives. Until the redemptive state, we can't be all reap and no sow. We have to remember when we sow through the hardships, the flip side of it is reaping the blessings. **Moshiach *prati*** (personal redemption) as well as *klali* (communal redemption) is brought on by each of us revealing Godliness in the world, to ourselves and to each other. The revelation at Sinai was from above; it was a temporal taste of what is to come, to bring Moshiach, which we can only do from within.

How we view and treat ourselves will not only affect our own happiness, but that of the entire world—we have to remove the layers of discontent and align with the faith that for each of us, all is for the ultimate good. One of my favorite lessons from Rabbi Simcha Bunim is: "Everyone must have two pockets and a note in each pocket, so that he or she can reach into one or the other, depending on the need. When feeling lowly and depressed, discouraged or disconsolate, one should reach into the right pocket and there find the words: *Bishvili nivra ha-olam*—**"The world was created for me."**[6] But when feeling high and mighty, one should reach into

the left pocket and find the words: *V'anochi afar v'efer*—**"I am but dust and ashes."**[7]

Revealing Oneness through Each One You Encounter

The Baal Shem Tov used to shiver when he would meet a new person. When asked why, he replied, "The Torah tells us, Love your neighbor like you love yourself (V'ahavta L'rey'echa Kamokha). People think 'rey'echa' means 'your neighbor', but it really means 'the one you are talking to', so you have to give your full heart to each person you are talking to." In order to reveal Hashem in the world, we need to uncover the pieces of holiness that are in each of us, one by one.

My dad was a Chaplain, a Rabbi in the Navy, and he traveled all over the world. On occasion, he would bump into Reb Shlomo Carlebach, who would sometimes tell him about the word **Shalom**. He said, "How can you say *Shalom* when you first meet someone and the same word when you say goodbye? *Shalom* comes from *shalem*—completeness. I was incomplete until I met you, but now that I met you, I am more complete than before. But, now that you are leaving, you are taking something away from me, and I say 'shalom' in the hope that someday you will come back and make me more complete again."

We are all made in the image of the Divine, and with each positive interaction, we see another piece of Hashem, and we feel more complete.

Carlebach taught a new generation of people who were far from Godliness about how to bring Divine awareness into their everyday lives. He reminded them that Hashem appeared to each of the *Avot* (our forefathers) as individuals—to Avraham alone, then Yitzchak, then Yakov—revealing Godself to each of them in the way that was best suited for their growth into their highest selves. So, we learn that every action, especially those we take toward **each individual we encounter is an opportunity for holy revelation.**

There is a famous story of the Talmudic sage Hillel, from the first century BCE, who moved to Israel to study Torah in Jerusalem with the great sages of the time, eventually becoming the *Nasi* (president) of the Sanhedrin (High Court). Much like Moshe, Hillel was very humble and, like Moshe, he looked up to Aharon, the High Priest, in the way that he conducted himself to "love peace and pursue peace, love all Hashem's creations and bring them close to the Torah."

The often repeated story of Hillel was originally recorded in Talmud Shabbat: a non-Jew had decided that he wanted to convert to Judaism, but would only do so if a Rabbi taught him the entire Torah while he stood on one foot. This person had gone to other Sages, but to no avail. Without giving up, he made his way to Hillel and asked the same. Hillel, with his great compassion and patience, replied, **"What is hateful to you, do not do to your neighbor.** That is the whole Torah: the rest is commentary —now go and study it!"

In this time of anxiety, self-doubt, self-hate, and depression, it seems that "Love your neighbor like you love yourself" may not be as strong a statement as "What is hateful to you, do not do to your neighbor." This teaches us not to do harm or treat the people around us in a negative way. Because even when we know we aren't being the best with ourselves, this *pasuk* reminds us that it is certainly best to not do it to anyone else, even if at times we are less than kind with ourselves. If the commandment is to love others as we love ourselves, and we feel that we don't have enough love for ourselves, then the only way to keep this *mitzvah* is to increase the love we have for ourselves and decrease the self-doubt and self-hate. Because if we don't show ourselves the proper love, how can we properly love others? And truly, the way we love ourselves *is* the way we will love others.

In *parashah* Tazria, we learn about **tzarot** (sad things), and that *tzarot* come from **lashon hara** (slander/negative speech), which means one is looking at people and oneself negatively. This **ayin hara** (evil eye) leads to *lashon hara*, which means looking at people with judgment, or incorrectly inferring that whatever they have is taking away from us; that there is not enough to go around. As we read these *parshiot*, we see the word **nega** (blemish/disease, נגע) repeated; a space which encompasses the lowest form of experience. The Ramban teaches the distinction between *nega* (disease, נגע) and **oneg** (pleasure, ענג) is only in a change of perspective. Hebrew is read from right to left, and in the word *nega* (נגע), you see the ayin (ע) is on the left. And, as the Rebbe Rashab taught the Frierdiker Rebbe, if we lead with *chesed (*loving kindness), we tap into the right side of the *sefirot* and our own beings, and look through the right eye, so to speak, the ayin (ע) of goodness leads. This is when we can move away from *nega* (נגע) and have oneg (pleasure, ענג), which is the highest form of life experience.[8]

Overcoming Self Doubt—Finding Faith in Hashem's Melody

As we know from the story of Exodus that we read every year over Pesach and in the parshiot, Hashem reminds Moshe that he can lead the nation, stand up to Pharaoh, and that anything he can imagine, he can manifest, as there is nothing the Infinite One cannot do, and any messenger of Hashem can will fate into physicality.

Imagine a world in which you had no self-doubts, you only saw the good, you only spoke positively, your faith was full and anxiety had no place. It seems we are further from that space than ever. But if Moshe, with a speech impediment, could become the speaker for the enslaved, freeing them from Pharaoh, we can become our own advocates to and for ourselves. The core teaching of Rebbe Nachman is the **Azamra**: teaching ourselves to rectify "harsh judgment" by finding the "good point" in ourselves and others and judging it favorably, thereby bringing merit to ourselves and others.

Music is born of the act of sifting through the bad notes to get to the good ones, as beautiful melodies are the various combinations of notes that go together melodically and harmoniously. This is the practice we have to continually perfect in our lives in order to remove the "bad" from ourselves and others. When that becomes second nature, we can reach a level where we don't see bad anymore—bringing ourselves to a place of *kulo tov* (all good); a place where we tune into all the melodies of life and allow them to lift us up.

Hashem reminds Moshe that whatever impingement he feels he has, it cannot impede him from his destiny, nor the people from redemption. Once Moshe was able to rid himself of his doubt and submit to his destiny, he was able to perform miracles. Of course miracles happen every moment, disguised as nature, but if we cloud them with doubt or anxiety, we can't see the miraculous good.

Delving further into the lesson of *Azamra*, it says, "And yet, in a little bit, the sinner is gone; you will contemplate his place, but he will not be there."[9] This correlates to the famous lesson in Pirkei Avot: **"Find yourself a teacher, acquire for yourself a friend, and judge every person favorably."** This practice of rectifying judgment is done by finding the good points in ourselves, since judgment is so often a projection of our own perceived lacking.

Judgment isn't intrinsically negative; it's needed in order to discern between good and less good decisions. But we have to find the sweet harmony, the *tiferet*, so that both judgment and fear can reveal good. Only when judgment takes over a person does it become a negative force, potentially resulting in anger and violence. That's why we meditate on God's Names and use our speech to moderate and mitigate judgment with mercy.

Suspending judgment in as many situations as possible is key. Often opposing views will bring about harsh judgements. But, as Reb Natan teaches in *Likutei Halachot*, all viewpoints derive from the **"Will of wills."** Although it is impossible to understand this rationally, if everyone tried to look at others from this perspective, then strife would cease. Conflict manifests when we fail to bind our will to the "Will of wills," because it is within that Will where harmony and peace prevail, since all is incorporated into the Oneness of the Light of Infinite.[10]

It's written, **"It is the nature of He who is good to do good."**[11] Balancing judgment with mercy, finding the sweet spot of harmony in ourselves and others is the way we can tap into the ultimate good, the Hidden Light, and bring that light, bit by bit, into this world of concealment, being a force of revelation and helping to usher in the final redemption.

Exile Is a State of Disconnect; Redemption Is the Rectification and the Reconnection

With Pharaoh, we see that after each plague he agrees that Hashem is the Almighty. But then he forgets, doubts, becomes faithless and fooled again; thinking he is in control and can save himself. When Moshe brings the next plague, he begs for it to stop and be reversed, saying that he will allow Moshe to take B'nei Yisrael out and serve God. But then the plague abates, and with it Pharaoh's compassion, and he hardens his heart again.

The Jews couldn't free themselves spiritually while in Egypt under Pharaoh. They needed to take action toward freeing themselves, not only spiritually but physically—from the space that had enslaved them and crushed their spirits. The first step was realizing that it is never too late to overcome one's circumstances and reach redemption, but to stay far from that which has enslaved us, it requires more than just the inspired epiphany. For each of us to actually be our true selves, we need to strip away the parts of us that are represented by *Mitzrayim* and cling to the parts of us that usher in redemption and our personal Promised Land.

All of the Torah's commandments are meant to take physicality and elevate it to spiritualize "reality." It is only when we act with the intent to unify ourselves with Divine consciousness that we can unify the animal and Godly souls within ourselves. ***Mitzrayim*** (מִצְרַיִם, Egypt) reflects *Meitzar* (מֵיצָר, a narrow constricted place), which is the definition of exile—spiritual narrowness and constriction. *Mitzrayim* is referred to as *ervat haaretz*, "the nakedness of the land,"[12] which is, of course, referring to the immorality that was rampant within it. Reb Natan explains that exile and immorality are bound together because the further one moves away from Godliness and holiness (which are beyond space), the more the person becomes entangled in space, i.e. exile. To serve and connect with The One, each person has to rise above immorality and transcend exile.[13]

When we read the stories of our people, we need to realize it's not just a historic retelling—these stories are perpetually played out within ourselves. We are all at times plagued with our own *Meitzar*, our own constrictions and enslavements, that which holds us back from reaching our potential and ascending to our personal Promised Lands. This is why the Lubavitcher Rebbe taught that the moment we stop leaving *Mitzrayim*, we are back there again. This is lifelong spiritual work.

If we jump back to the beginning, from Adam and Eve, and the breaking of the Edenic state to the state that we find ourselves in—our struggle, our task and indeed our purpose is to spiritualize reality by bringing light into our own darkness (*prati*), and by doing so, to bring light into the world (*klali*). By continuously doing this and focusing on the light, and elevating the dark fallen sparks, we grab the heel of the other side, and bring it to the side of truth. "Truth when pursued will always wash away faithlessness and falsehood," as it's written in Shoftim. *Justice, justice shall you pursue, that you may live and possess the land the Lord, your God, is giving you.*[14] This is because truth and justice are how we merit to stay alive and settle the Promised Land. This isn't only referring to Israel, but the ways that each of us can reach personal redemption. And healing our own broken hearts heals the larger broken heart of the entire world.

GREET ALL HATE WITH LOVE

"The best fighter is never angry." —Lao Tzu

Being unhappy is a vicious cycle. It can lead to worry, anxiety, anger, depression. Each of these can trigger any of the others. Anger is toxic to your body and soul, often triggering one's 'fight or flight' response, which floods the body with stress hormones (e.g. adrenaline and cortisol.) This could manifest in all sorts of health, nervous system, and digestive problems. The cure for all this is easier said than done but it begins with a healthy perspective, with trust and faith that all is for the ultimate good and that everything will work out according to the Divine design.

I went through periods of depression when everything in my life was seemingly good. I wasn't poor or friendless or in dire straits, but in the way I viewed my life, I might as well have been. The Talmud teaches that a person is led down the path that they choose to follow.[15] If they believe everything is for the good, then reality becomes good, but if that person only sees "bad", then they are treated accordingly. In this way, we truly are cocreators of reality.

I broke this cycle for myself when I realized that if everything around me is good, but I can still get myself into such a dark place, then the opposite must be true—I can get myself to the light, no matter what circumstances I find myself in. It was then that I tried to become light, just as when light from your own flame is shared with another and your flame doesn't diminish, but ignites another. Since then I have tried to live by what John Mayer so beautifully asks for in his singing on *Gravity*, "**Just keep me where the light is**". Doing so is rooted in giving—love and belief in yourself and others. This creates more love and builds community, which every person needs to feel alive.

Peace Is the Vessel That Contains Every Blessing

The Maharal explains that whomever truly trusts in Hashem will be blessed with a happy disposition; teaching that where there is complete faith, there is no room for anger, for there is great joy. This relates to Rebbe Nachman's famous teaching, "***Ein shum yeush ba'olam klal!***", which means, "There is no such thing as despair in the world, at all!' It's a hard thing to put faith into, especially when we feel like everything is horrible and hopeless. But we have to hold onto our faith and when we see the good that comes from this struggle, then we'll know why we had to experience it. Life must be lived, lessons must be learned, and, in the end, good often comes from "bad." The *Zohar* teaches: "By (the way one handles one's) anger, one can recognize who one is. If a person guards their soul at a moment of anger and does not allow it (one's soul) to be torn from its place...this is a person who is as they should be...This is a complete person."[16]

The Lubavitcher Rebbe explains that on the second day of creation, Hashem did not say, "And it was good,"[17] because the firmament—division—was created on that day. It wasn't until the third day that Hashem said "it was good" and included the second day in this blessing, since the firmament had been purified, healing the division it created the day before. This teaches us that constriction and concealment create division, leaving us with the task to reunite all of the elements that were once whole. Our entire purpose is to take the fallen sparks of disunity and elevate them to their source, the Infinite Light itself.

In the Talmud it says that anger can cause a sage to lose his wisdom or a person who is destined for greatness to forfeit it.[18]

'*Shalom*' means peace, '*shalem*' means complete, so we are only complete when we are at peace. Peace only comes from mindful joy which never has the space for anger.

The Alter Rebbe teaches that when hatred rises in a person's mind towards another (or jealousy, anger, or a grudge) one should immediately remove this thought from the mind and not entertain it. On the contrary, the person should prevail over their emotions, treating this person with kindness, and showing an abundance of love. Not only should one not take revenge, but on the contrary, should repay the offender with good, as we learn from the *Zohar*.[19]

Just the other week I thought about greeting all hate with love and seeing how life changes. In parashat Korach, we read of him and his faction's dissent against Moshe. Moshe, knowing the truth and fully capable of setting them straight, chose not to go on the defensive or offensive. It's written, "Moshe heard and fell [to the ground] on his face."[20] In *Likkutey Moharan*, a few lessons before the *Azamra*, Rabbeinu shares a powerful analogy[21] about the earth and dirt and what we can learn from them. Rebbe Nachman explains how the earth represents *bitul* (nullification) and how it gives life and therefore also represents love. He teaches that when a person encounters opposition, they shouldn't take a stand against their "enemy" saying, "what they do to me, I will repay in kind." Because it is this disposition that exacerbates the situation and causes the enemy to achieve their goal; where they see the person respond and act exactly in the manner they were hoping to provoke. Rabbeinu teaches that a person should respond in the opposite manner, to judge their "enemy" favorably—turning a bad situation into a good one.

It's written in Talmud Brachot, "**Let my soul be like earth to everyone.**"[22] Everyone treads on the earth and destroys it to an extent, yet the earth remains in its humble state and continues to provide nourishment, food, drink, gold, silver and precious stones. Rabbeinu teaches that in the case of the enemy that may oppose us or treat us poorly, we need to do for them every good—just like the earth. As King Solomon teaches, "If your enemy is hungry, feed him bread, if he is thirsty, give him water to drink."[23] It should be noted that this is speaking in the case of strife and conflict and not, God forbid, if someone is in grave danger, in which case they need to take a stand, alert the authorities or find a safe space away from their antagonist.

In the space of the conflict that many of us face from opposition throughout life, this is a lesson of how we can flip the "bad" into good. In such a case, Rabbeinu shares a beautiful analogy where the antagonist is our neighbor and is digging a tunnel under the house. When they're halfway, we will likely default to wanting to treat them in kind and get to them before we are gotten to. But if we do that, we've just done half of the job for them. If, however, we look at the earth as *bitul* and nurturing love—that which opposes hate—and go inside, pouring the earth on our side of the house, then overturning the other person's plan, this makes it that much harder for the antagonist to use anger towards resolution.

Rabbeinu teaches that taking a stand against the enemy or working against them is akin to digging just like the enemy, making it that much easier for them to reach their goals. Instead, by tapping into the aspect of earth and of, "Let my soul be like earth…," we overturn the enemy's plans, and as it's written in Proverbs, "He who digs a pit will fall into it."[24] The antagonist falls and remains in their own pit that they dug for themselves because of the earth (love) poured on top of the hate.[25] Bringing it back to Korach, and his rebellion, as is stated in the Talmud, his controversy was not *Lishmah*, for the sake man of Heaven, and he was not *mevatel* (nullified) at all. So, he and his faction were swallowed up by the earth. We have to remember in the end it will all be good, as King Solomon writes in Kohelet, "God sides with the persecuted."[26]

In addition, as Rambam citing Chazal teaches, someone who gets angry is like one who worships idols.[27] As we learn in Tanya, when we are angered by an action or event, we are temporarily denying *Hashgacha Pratit* (Divine providence), which is really what enabled that action to happen.[28]

Responsa from the Lubavitcher Rebbe are always inspiring and seem to be applicable way beyond the person in question. This particular passage jumps out as an example of advice that should be implemented into universal practice:

> *Keep the mitzvah found in the Shulchan Aruch [Code of Jewish Law], that if you hurt someone's feelings—even out of anger—you must apologize in person and ask for complete forgiveness.*
>
> *It is by nature difficult for a person to apologize. Nevertheless, you should overcome that difficulty and do it.*
>
> *In that way, every time you are about to get angry, you will*

remember that afterwards you will have to brace yourself and ask for forgiveness... That itself will help you weaken your tendency towards anger.[29]

Furthermore, Rebbe Nachman teaches that Hashem's light, which descends upon us, is in an undifferentiated and unformed—i.e. sealed—state. It is up to each of us to create a vessel with which to receive this light, so that it can take shape within and through us. If a person's vessel is faulty, it doesn't mean the light won't come to them, but that they won't have the capacity to shape it into a blessing. It is up to each person to perfect their vessel so that they may take Hashem's blessing.[30] We cannot choose our blessings or how much Light we will receive, but we can continually work to make ourselves vessels that are open to receiving—and giving—blessings and Light. This is what it means to *be* a blessing.

We can use speech to either bless or curse. Our rituals connected to the Torah give us so many opportunities to bless. Every day, multiple times a day, the Siddur guides us to say אֲדֹנָי שְׂפָתַי תִּפְתָּח וּפִי יַגִּיד תְּהִלָּתֶךָ, **"O Lord, open my lips, and let my mouth declare Your praise."**[31] In *Talmud Berakhot*, Rabbi Yoḥanan says that before every prayer one should recite this verse and when they finish praying, they should say, "May the words of my mouth and the meditations of my heart be acceptable before You."[32] Existing in the space of gratitude is essential to creating a vessel that can receive one's proper share of the Infinite Light.

Coming from a place of darkness and a desire to bring a people down through cursing them will only bring harm to oneself. That is the lesson of the verse, "Those who bless shall be blessed".[33] If you are one who gives blessings, it means you are a vessel for blessings. The potential for Light is limitless for such a person, as good begets good and blessings beget blessings. This verse illuminates how dangerous it is to connect with the *sitra achra* (the other side). A curse is not something that a person can hope for as a one time thing. We can't wish ill on someone and not be affected by it. Cursing another, trying to break another's vessel, is a fracturing of one's own vessel.

We have to greet hate with love, and use every instance as an opportunity to heal our fractured vessels, reconnecting to the spirit of blessing, pushing away the *sitra achra*, and inviting in the Light of the Infinite.

THE SECRET TO LOVE: DIVINE CONCEALING AND REVEALING

The great Rabbi Akiva taught that the fundamental principle of the Torah is to 'Love your neighbor as yourself.'[34] Many ask if that is possible, when our default is selfishness and making sure first and foremost that we are taken care of before thinking of anyone else. The Baal Shem Tov expounds on Rabbi Akiva's lesson: though we are aware of our many faults, we still look out for and love ourselves, and we need to do the same for those around us despite their faults. We need to uplift and elevate, which can only be done when leading with love of the "neighbor as yourself."

Ahava (ah-ha-va)/אהבה/love. In Hebrew, the root word for *'love'* is *'hav'* which means *"to give"*. Loving is synonymous with giving—as real love is created. As The Beatles say, *"The love you take is equal to the love you make."*

You see this most clearly in the love a parent gives to their child. As a baby, the child's existence fully depends on the parent giving of themselves at every moment. This tireless giving creates an attachment stronger than any other kind—profound, unconditional love. So the greater the giving, the deeper the love.

Ahava has the same gematria (numerical value)—13—as the word

Echad (the Hebrew word for 'one'). And so to reach oneness and love, we have to be in tune with each other and ourselves, and when we share our oneness and our love, that is 13 + 13, which is 26. And as many of us know, 26 is the numerical value of Hashem's four-letter name (the Tetragrammaton), the ultimate Divine Infinite Light.

When we read the famous verse, "**And you shall love the Lord your God**,"[35] we are left asking, how can it be that we are commanded to feel? This is especially curious for people that tend to believe that love is a sensation that magically, spontaneously occurs. It may be because this way of thinking is so prevalent that Erich Fromm writes in "The Art of Loving", "There is hardly any activity, any enterprise, which is started with such tremendous hopes and expectations, and yet, which fails so regularly, as love." To illuminate the verse from the Torah, our sages point out that it's not an abstract feeling that is being presented to us, but rather the command to act lovingly, and by this act, love will be created. Love is a choice, and an action. In this way, the commandment, "And you shall love" manifests through all the ways in which we perform acts of love in the world.

In his TED Talk, Rabbi Lord Jonathan Sacks suggested to his audience that they run a *Search-and-Replace* operation on the texts of their minds and substitute every instance of the word *"self"* with the word *"other."* So instead of trying to do *"self-help,"* you would do *"other-help;"* instead of looking after your *"self-esteem,"* you would look after *"others'-esteem."* He went on to say that, *"If you do that, you will begin to feel the power of one of the most moving sentences in all of religious literature: Though I walk through the valley of the shadow of death, I will fear no evil, for you are with me."*[36]

When we feel isolated and cut off from love, it can feel like darkness all around. The *Zohar* teaches that darkness isn't an entity unto itself, it is the absence of light. Thus, a little bit of light, a little bit of love, will illuminate a lot of darkness.

Just as important as the act of giving is the sincerity and love in which it is given. If our heart compels us to want to hold on and not let go, it is the act of giving and letting go that we must master. All of life is about loving and creating love for others, which always brings to mind what the Lubavitcher Rebbe said so beautifully, "You already belong. You are already holy. You are already loved. Now you too must love, and by loving, help others feel that they also belong."

Many of us have heard that we are one nation and also one Torah scroll, in which each individual is a letter. Thus we are interdependent, equally important, and ultimately, one. David Sacks, one of my favorite humans, a writer and producer of *The Simpsons*, frequent presenter at my Don't Block Your Blessings festival, and creator of the podcast Spiritual Tools for an Outrageous World, explains that each letter, and each one of us, is a musical note and that our task is to live in harmony by being in tune and tuning each other. We should strive to not be dissonant. He gives the analogy of someone sitting at a beautiful piano and playing the black and white keys and it not sounding right, wondering what's wrong, and just then someone else comes to tune that piano. Suddenly, it all sounds gorgeous. The piano is beautiful and what was being played had the potential of beauty, but it needed to be in tune. That's our mission—we need to uplift each other, judge each other favorably and show love to one another.

If you focus on others as you would yourself, then you will love yourself more and, by virtue of that, become love for others.

Stay Giving: The Kabbalistic Path to Receive

Kabbalistically, the letters that spell out the Divine name represent aspects of our inner consciousness: the upper *heh* (ה) represents our desire to give and the lower *heh* (ה) our desire to receive. Our infinite Source perpetually gives without the need to receive – this correlates to and is mirrored in the extent to which we can give unconditionally.

Thus, the lower *heh* (ה) ascending to the upper *heh* (ה) represents our spiritual awakening to pure giving and unconditional love. This inner transformation when manifested enables us to experience the infinite goodness that is the source of all reality.

The lower *heh* (ה) is empty because if we focus simply on receiving, we are hollow; the upper *heh* is full, like a cup overflowing inviting all to drink. When we recognize the bestowing nature of the universe, which sustains life at every single moment without asking for anything in return, we discover that by emulating this and becoming beings who give unconditionally, we achieve balance and deeper levels of Divine union. We thereby unite the lower *heh* with the upper *heh*.

It's only when we attach ourselves in such a way to our Source, through learning the Torah and keeping the *mitzvot lishmah*, that we can become love and light and manifest blessings for ourselves and each other.

don't trip
on the finite
minutia

don't take
ad nauseam

just
give
love
live

the world
is infinite

and

gives
to the giving

loves the
truly living

and

shines light
on the ones who create
space for it.

spiritualize reality

There was a time when I stopped visiting Israel because it was too difficult for me to go there after my *savta* (grandmother) passed away. Her house had always been my first stop. I would run there directly from Ben Gurion airport. She would likely have some Yemenite food and mind-blowing schnitzel awaiting my arrival. Back when I was in Yeshiva and lived in Yerushalayim, I would take my friends to my savta's in Ramat Gan for Shabbatot (they all called her Grandma). I remember her waking up at 5 am every day, covering her head and saying the morning prayers. She would cook Yemenite food and Moroccan salads, and my friends and I would sing Shabbat songs in Hebrew, as she sat on the couch crying from happiness. It's incredible to realize all the time that she and her family were exiled in Yemen and Ethiopia. But eventually they were able to come back to Israel, and she could see her grandson living in Yerushalayim, singing the songs that have been sung throughout history every Shabbat since the Jews left Egypt. She made it, we made it—the yearning for home and the unification of a people with its ancestral homeland was realized in her lifetime.

Yemenite Jews are unique in that they are our strongest link to the *Beit HaMikdash* (Holy Temple). They settled in Yemen while the Temple still stood and have maintained their Hebrew pronunciations and Jewish practices in a completely unique way. Whereas most every other Jewish tribe has traveled and assimilated into the larger cultures around them, Yemenite Jews have stayed in Yemen up until the last hundred or so years. Even the great Eastern European *Gadol V'Posek HaDor* Rabbi Moshe Feinstein said that the Yemenite Jews pronunciation of Hebrew is closest to that of Moshe Rabbeinu.

Concepts in Kabbalah

Now to the *parashah*, which centers around the *Beit HaMikdash* and its practices, and how these pertain to our lives.

The Hebrew word *kabbalah* means "parallel" or "correspondence." So Kabbalah is the mystical teaching of the parallels and correspondences between all of creation and the Divine power that creates it. The structures of the four letters of the Divine Name (Havayah) express the Creative Force that sustains and is manifested in all levels of reality. We explored this notion in Vayakhel's *dvar*, when we spoke about the parallels between Hashem's "arousal from above" and our "arousal from below."

This was illustrated two millennia ago in the sacrificial rituals of the *Beit HaMikdash*. The Temple is a microcosm of the creation and all the rituals performed in it are both symbolic of and actualizations of the Divine service each of us is tasked with in the physical world.

The Arizal explains that Hashem created five kingdoms in our physical world: the "silent" i.e. inanimate or mineral, the vegetable, the animal, the "articulate" i.e. humans, and, finally, the soul. Each of these is a world unto itself, and each is also a projection of the one that precedes it at a lower spiritual level. This structure of the physical world reflects the structure of the highest spiritual realm, *atzilut*, a world of pure "emanation."

In the process of creating all of the worlds below *atzilut*, a shattering happened. Out of *tohu*, "chaos," came Divine sparks which infused themselves within all aspects of reality in all the lower worlds, including the lowest, which is our physical world. Kabbalah explains that the other fundamental aspect of the creation of the world is *tikkun*, meaning "rectification" or "repair." When we use any element of our physical world for a Divine purpose, we elevate the spark within it to its holy source, turning the physical *back* into the spiritual.[1]

The Soul's Sacrifice of the Animal Within

Now that we have a bit of the kabbalistic background, we can jump into the actual words in this week's *parashah*, Vayikra. The portion begins: "When one among you offers a sacrifice to God...".[2]

Immediately, we ask, what sort of sacrifice? Why? And how? King David, whose son built the first Temple, writes in Tehillim, "For You [God] do *not* desire sacrifices; else I would give it: You do *not* delight in burnt offering. The sacrifice of God is a broken spirit. A broken and contrite heart, O God, You will not despise."[3]

Animal sacrifices were a way for ancient Jews to elevate themselves spiritually, but the sacrifices would have been meaningless if they weren't done with true intention and a full heart to heal oneself and the harms one has done. King David writes that God will not despise a "broken spirit", because true remorse makes a person feel broken, and true repentance comes from the desire to be connected to Hashem again, in order to be whole. In order to achieve this level of return, *teshuvah,* we were commanded to bring a sacrifice in the time of the Temple, just as we are now commanded to pray, in the absence of the Temple.

The Hebrew word for sacrifice is *korban* which comes from the word *karov* or *lekarev* meaning "close" or "to come closer." It's written in the *pasuk,* מִכֶּם, which means yourself, implying the one who is offering the *korban*, is sacrificing themself. I love how Rabbi Lord Jonathan Sacks puts it:

> *Vayikra is about why love needs law and law needs love. It is about the quotidian acts of devotion that bring two beings close, even when one of them is vaster than the universe and the other is a mortal of flesh and blood. It is about being human, sinning, falling short, always conscious of our fragile hold on life, yet seeking to come close to God and—what is sometimes harder—allowing Him to come close to us.*[4]

In the last chapter, we discussed Hashem's dwelling in the sanctuary representing the deeper dwelling amongst each and every one of us. In this *parashah*, the Torah teaches how the holy priests are guided in their service and sacrifice in the sanctuary of the past.

The *korbanot* are a beautiful and spiritual ritual—picture the elements surrounding the sacrifice, with the presence of the *kohanim* (priests) accompanied by the chanting and songs of the *levi'im*, the (Levites). The Zohar teaches that the service of the *kohanim* was in silence, with the devotion of the heart, signifying *hamshachah* (drawing forth, from Above), while the service of the *levi'im* was with song and music, signifying *hala'ah* (sublimation; elevating from below upwards).[5] As it's written, "The Kohanim in their silent service and their desire drew [God's presence] downwards and the Levites in their songs and praises drew [the human soul and sacrifice] upwards."[6] This is mirrored in how we tend to the sanctuaries within our own souls; the inner acts of sacrifice we practice each day, the desire we have to bring holiness down from above, and the artfulness we use to draw our spirits and surroundings upward.

Vayikra lists a variety of *korbanot* (sacrifices) to be brought by the individual and the community. Below are some general categories:

Olah (burnt offering, עלה) – an animal sacrifice that is completely burnt upon the altar.

Minchah (meal-offering, מנחה) – an offering a fine flower, oil, and frankincense

Shelamim (peace-offering, שלמים) – a fire-offering of the fats and kidneys of an animal; the other parts are given to the *Kohen*, and the remainder is eaten by the owner.

Chatat (sin-offering, חטאת) – the blood of the animal is poured upon the Altar and the fats are also burnt; the rest is eaten by the *Kohanim*.

Asham (guilt-offering, אשם) – depending on the individual's means, this offering may be either an animal from the flock, two doves, or fine flour.

Milu'im (inauguration-offering, מלואים) – an offering brought by a *Kohen* when he joins the service in the Bait HaMikdash.

Korban Todah (thanksgiving-offering, קרבן תודה) – an animal sacrifice brought together with four different types of bread; some parts of the animals are burnt upon the Altar, others are given to the *Kohen*, and the remainder is eaten by the owner.

Korban tamid (daily sacrifice, קרבן תמיד) – every morning and afternoon, the Kohanim in the *Mishkan* (Tabernacle) and later in the *Bait HaMikdash*, brought a fire-offering of a yearling lamb together with fine flour and oil.

Ketoret (incense-offering, קטרת) – an offering of eleven finely ground spices, which were burnt upon the Golden Altar in the Inner Sanctuary, next to the Holy of Holies.[7]

There are two concrete ways in which we could, to some extent, simulate bringing a *korban*. In Talmud Menachot it teaches, based on 'This is the law of the sin offering,'[8] that anyone who engages in studying the law of the sin offering is ascribed credit as though he sacrificed a sin offering.[9] Aside from learning the laws, there is a custom to recite פרשת הקרבנות (*parashat hakorbanot*) as part of our daily *tefillah*, specifically saying:

אם נתחיבתי חטאת, שתהא אמירה זו מרצה לפניך כאלו הקרבתי חטאת

—"If I am obliged to bring a sin-offering (or any other kor-
ban), may it be Your will that the recitation of the portion
dealing with חטאת *should be considered as if I brought the*
sin-offering."

Of Yourself with Love

The Alter Rebbe breaks down the *pasuk*—אָדָם' כִּי־יַקְרִיב מִכֶּם קָרְבָּן לָה'—
Adam ki yakriv—"If a man desires to *draw close* to Divinity, then
mikem korban laHashem,[10] you must offer *of yourself."* The word
mikem signifies the offering of the *nefesh elokit* (our Divine soul)
and, further in the *pasuk*, the phrase "of the animals..." signifies the
"animal' in man's heart (the *nefesh habahamit*—the animal soul)—
from the animal within one's base characteristics. The Lubavitcher
Rebbe expounds on this lesson, explaining that the ultimate purpose
for a person is not an *avodah* (service) relating to the Divine soul,
for its own sake, but rather to achieve a *birur*, a refinement of the
animal soul which we see in the word *mikem* (of you) followed by
korban leHashem (an offering to God). We see in the sentence, "If
any man brings an offering *of* you...": to draw close to God, one
must make a sacrifice *of* "you", of oneself. So, "you" is the essential
element of a holy sacrifice—from the heart, from one's godly soul,
turning good intention into good action.

The words 'from the heart,' mean that the person has to bring the
sacrifice willingly. It is the same with *tefillah*, we should pray out
of love not obligation. The same applies with lending money and
other matters "between man and his fellow," which are meant to be
performed willingly and even *b'simchah* (with joy). The Bartinura
comments on Talmud Avot regarding giving *tzedakah* (charity):
if someone were to do it with their "face pressed to the ground"
(under duress), it would be as though the person didn't give
the *tzedakah* at all. The person will still receive a reward for the
mitzvah, but, in a sense, it is as though the person didn't perform

it because they did it purely out of obligation instead of willingly and lovingly.[11]

The second part of the *pasuk* (verse) pertains to an animal sacrifice, meaning one's animal soul. As it's written, "...from animals—from cattle or from the flock shall you bring your offering."[12] This relates to the physical body, physical desires, the natural world, so it is the physical sacrifice—actually giving up the animal (or its modern equivalent)—with the purpose to sanctify and redirect the "animal" in man. The Rebbe explains that when the animal in man is harnessed in the service of God it has the power to take him closer to God than his Godly soul alone could reach. The greater the sacrifice, the greater the reward.

Reb Natan teaches that a person's sin is due to their lack of *da'at*. As it's written, "A person sins only because a spirit of foolishness overcame him."[13] To rectify this lack of *da'at*, the person must bring an animal sacrifice which reflects that lack. In this way, the person demonstrates their readiness to sacrifice their animalistic tendencies.[14] We learn that the animal sacrifices in particular have the power to rectify the lowest worlds[15] and that the *korbanot* in general correspond to the Act of Creation, when Hashem separated good from "bad." In the same way the *korbanot* separate good from evil.[16]

The Three Soul-Garments

In the same way that any animal that is to become a *korban* cannot have a blemish, we are tasked with not having blemishes in regards to the "animal" within ourselves. This is done through self-examination and true remorse; searching one's soul for rifts in the unity of one's being; this includes the three soul-garments of thought, speech and deed. If a kosher animal was torn apart by a predator, it would then be deemed unkosher, *treif,* which literally means "torn." Unlike an animal deemed *treif*, however, *we* are able to do full repentance, which in Hebrew is called *teshuvah*, meaning "to return." We are never completely torn away from God. This *parashah* teaches us the process of taking the *sitra achra*, the fallen sparks, and elevating them into light, supplementing the darkness. But this can only be done through both of our inclinations, for good and for evil. This is the meaning of the famous passage, "And you shall love the Eternal, your God, with *all* your heart."[17] Our most profound sacrifice is when we subdue and harness the overwhelming power of the evil inclination and manage to use that energy for the highest good, in Divine service.

The Zohar states this clearly, "When the *sitra achra* are subdued below [in our lower world], the Holy One, blessed be He, is exalted above and is aggrandized in His glory. In fact, there is no worship of God except when it issues forth from darkness, and no good except when it proceeds from evil… The perfection of all things is attained when the intermingled good and evil become totally good, for there is no good except if it issues out of evil. By that good His glory rises, and that is the perfect worship."[18]

This is seen in the "Parable of the Harlot," in which a king instructs his son to lead an exemplary and moral life and not to fall into temptation. Meanwhile, the king secretly tasks a temptress to seduce his son, thereby testing his son's devotion to him. The woman tries everything to seduce the prince, but he rejects all attempts. At this, his father, the king, rejoices and bestows all his honor and greatest gifts to his son, the prince. The Zohar means to illustrate that all the glory due to the prince was brought about by the temptress! "Surely she is to be praised on all accounts, for, firstly, she fulfilled the king's command and secondly, she caused the son to receive all that good and led to that intense love of the king for his son."[19] Conquering the evil within ourselves demonstrates our truest devotion to the Infinite One.

As you read through the *parashah*, you will notice that the sacrifices are meant to create "… an aroma that is pleasing to God." Not only must each person bring the sacrifice to Hashem with a full heart, but each slaughtered animal must be "fit" to be sacrificed, so that it is pleasing to the Holy One. As above, so below: when preparing and *shechting* an animal for us to eat, the animal must be fit, i.e. kosher. The Jewish laws and rituals for this are very specific and strict, and even after the animal is slaughtered properly and in a humane way, it is still inspected to see that there are no fatal lesions on the lungs. These are all aspects of the animal being "fit" or kosher. In regards to *us* being "fit," we must eat as a means to serve Hashem, being mindful of that as its purpose. When our food is elevated into holiness, then the life it came from and our lives are elevated. So, our sages teach that a person's "table is like an altar." This is why on Shabbat we salt the challah, just as the sacrifices were salted. Shabbat is a taste of the world to come, and prayer is a taste and a mirroring of the rituals we once carried out in the Temple.

But if we have intention without action, or action without heart, then the "aroma" we create is not pleasing and the sparks are not fully elevated. My prayer and blessing is that we mirror the upper realms in this physical world, that we liberate and elevate all the fallen sparks, so that the world can reach its maximum spiritual potential that is pleasing on the highest level to ourselves and to Hashem—so much so that the final redemption reveals itself speedily.

when the screens
of separation fall

Radiant is the world soul,

Full of splendor and beauty,

Full of life,

Of souls hidden,

Of treasures of the holy spirit,

Of fountains of strength,

Of greatness and beauty.

Proudly I ascend

Toward the heights of the world soul

That gives life to the universe.

How majestic the vision –

Come, enjoy,

Come, find peace,

Embrace delight,

Taste and see that God is good.

Why spend your substance on what does not nourish

And your labor on what cannot satisfy?

Listen to me, and you will enjoy what is good,

And find delight in what is truly precious.

These poetic words are from the notebook of Rav Kook.[1]

This week's *parashah*, Tzav, continues discussing the intricacies of the Temple sacrifices and touches on *chametz* (leavened bread). It's the *parashah* before Pesach/Passover (some years it's read on the Shabbat just prior, and other years we read it right after Purim, a few weeks before). Learning the *parashah*, we can draw connections between Leviticus/Vayikra and the larger Jewish story of moving from constriction into spiritual freedom and expansion; from *safek* (doubt) into salvation. So when Tzav falls out such that we have a few weeks before Pesach to get into the mindset of redemption, I see it as a blessing. As Rav Kook so eloquently asks of us all, "Find delight in what is truly precious."

My dad[2] was a Rabbi and Chaplain in the Navy, so we celebrated Pesach all over the world, including Japan and Italy. Whenever possible, he would invite military personnel to the Seder, as well as friends and family. My dad grew up in a kosher home and attended services, but was not fully observant until he started studying in yeshiva during his second year in Jerusalem. He also met my mom (*a"h*) and her Yemenite family at that time and took on some of their customs—not the thick, soft Yemenite matzah that looks like a pita or the *kitniyot* (Hebrew for legumes), but he would allow *kitniyot* at the table to show that it is kosher and part of the tradition to some, even though he personally didn't eat it.

In college, and later when I moved to Crown Heights with my ex, I was exposed to Chabad's Pesach customs through her family. To them, it's important not to eat any *gebrokts* (Yiddish for matzah that has come in contact with water) during the seven days of Pesach. So I would have to sneakily dip my matzah into the chicken soup bowl, because that was always one of my favorite things to do. Incidentally, my mom's Yemenite tradition is to wrap the matzah in a wet cloth and always eat it wet and soft.

It's only recently that I really began to delve into the meaning of Pesach. I've realized that the Seder is not just a *historical* retelling of the Jews' exodus from Egypt, but an actual manifestation, an opportunity for each of us to leave our own Egypts. Through this ritual, we're meant to free ourselves, to 'burn' the *chametz* that holds us back from seeing and living in full truth *(emet)*, from being fully connected to the Infinite Light *(ohr ha-kodesh)*. As it's written in the Zohar, "G-d does not dwell in... a fragmented place."[3]

In his notebook, Rav Kook also writes:

> *"The reality of Hashem's providence is discernible when the world is seen in its totality. The Divine presence is not manifest in anything defective. Since Hashem does not abide where there is deficiency, how can Hashem abide where everything is lacking, where all we have is the weak and puny entity, only the particularity of the ego?*
>
> *This call to be committed always to the principle of universality to the divine ensemble, where all things have their being, is the essence of the soul of the righteous who walk before Hashem and whose delight is in the Divine."*[4]

We must remember through the story of our enslavement that we, too, were once slaves and that, as Dr. King reminds us, no one is free until we are all free. Redemption is when the light of universality shines. It's our task to usher in that revelation. This starts within our own sanctuaries and emanates from there; nullifying the ego so the screens of separation between us all begin to fall. Indeed, the Alter Rebbe teaches in the Tanya that the basis and root purpose of the entire Torah is to elevate and exalt the soul high above the body to [G-d], the source and root of all worlds, and to draw down the *Ein Sof* (Infinite Light). Only when we place primary importance of soul over body can the walls that separate us come down and be replaced with love and unification—since it's our bodies that separate us from each other, while our souls bind us together. When one focuses on the body, the separation between us becomes apparent, and only the love we create can bind us, but a created love can never equal a natural and innate love. So, love between people whose primary importance is focused on the physical, on the body over the soul, is based on external factors and endures as long as those factors remain in play. Only when we shift our focus towards the soul over the body, of oneness over self, of the unifying and Infinite Light of the Creator of all creation, over the differences of the elements of creation, can Infinite Love exist in its purest state.[5]

The Biyur of Haughtiness

In this week's *parashah*, Hashem provides the instructions for the priestly meal offerings—sacrifices that did not involve animals. Moses is told that "[the meal offering] shall not be baked leavened (*lo teahfeh chametz*). I have presented it as their share from My fire-offerings."[6] In Exodus/Shemot, when Hashem gives the commandments of Pesach, it's written, "No leaven (*chametz)* shall be found in your houses for seven days. For whoever eats what is *chametz*, that person shall be cut off from the community of Israel, whether he is a stranger or a citizen of the country."[7]

Chametz literally means leavening: that which causes bread to rise. Chazal (our Sages of blessed memory) teach us that this *chametz* represents arrogance and the evil inclination, the *yetzer hara*. In Talmud *Berachot*, the *yetzer hara* is depicted as the "yeast in the dough",[8] puffing up a person's pride. The Talmud explains that the portion of the meal-offering eaten by the priest (*kohen*) is not allowed to be offered on the altar (*mizbeach*). A priest is dependent on Divine Gifts for their bread, so they cannot succumb to haughtiness or arrogance. But lay people have to work for their bread (with the "sweat of their brow" after Adam's sin). The more wealth they accumulate, the more the evil inclination manifests in the form of ego, haughtiness, and arrogance. Rebbe Nachman talks about *taavat mammon* (the lust for money), explaining that it is most apparent in a person who makes it their life's mission to amass great wealth.[9] Lacking *emunah*, faith in Hashem, they instead puts their trust (*bitachon*) in money, mistakenly believing that the more they have, the more secure and fulfilling life will be—they are in complete control of their own destiny.

As you may know, Jews are prohibited from consuming *chametz* during the seven days of Pesach. But we are also obligated to search our homes in preparation for the holiday, collecting any leftover scraps and crumbs that might be hidden, and then to ritually burn them before *Pesach* begins. This process is called *biyur*.

The ritual primes us to spend *Pesach* ridding ourselves of our spiritual *chametz*—our arrogance and pride. It's important to face ourselves honestly as we do this, and, like the practice of *biyur*, there comes a time to let our egos "burn," to not let them hold us back any longer so that we can strengthen our *emunah* (faith) and connect to something higher than ourselves.

The *Yehi Ratzon* that we recite after the burning of the *chametz* reads:

> "Just as I have eliminated the chametz from my house and from all I possess, may it be desirable before You, the One Who Brings Being into Being, God to me and God to my ancestors, to rid me of the Evil Inclination. May I be privileged enough to have that urge burnt from the depths of my heart until it is no more than smoke. And so, too, may You, like the very wind of destruction, rid by fire all wickedness from the land."

Incidentally, the search (*bedikat*) for the *chametz* may not be done by sunlight or moonlight, and is only valid by the light of a candle. It is the same with the search within our own *yetzer hara*—it can only be done with the light of the *neshamah* (soul) which is called *ner* (candle). As it says in Proverbs, "The candle of Hashem is the soul of man, which searches the chambers of one's inner being."[10]

Matzah—the central symbol of Pesach—is the antithesis of *chametz*. It is known as *lechem oni*, the bread of poverty and affliction.[11] Matzah signifies the humility that comes with poverty, and so the *mitzvah* (obligation) to eat matzah can only truly be fulfilled if it is eaten with humility. The matzah that the Israelites ate in Egypt was *lechem oni*, and so, too, the matzah that we eat over Pesach reminds us to be humble—to *bitul hayesh*, to negate and nullify all traces of ego and self-centeredness, in order to transcend the illusion of a separate self.

It's no coincidence that matzah (מַצָּה) and *chametz* (חָמֵץ) are both composed of the same letters. The only difference is that matzah is spelled with a *hey* (ה) and *chametz* with a *chet* (ח). We see that the letter *chet* (ח) is completely closed from three sides, symbolizing that "sin crouches at the entrance,"[12] while the *hey* (ה) has an opening on top, which means there is always an opening above, indicating the possibility to return to the Light. As our Sages say, "'Open for Me as little as the eye of the needle, and I will open for you like the entrance to a hall." Rebbe Nachman teaches that each and every person, even the most wicked, must find the one good point in themselves, and that one point, however small, can bring them to merit in Goodness itself. As we see in Talmud *Kiddushin*, just one single thought of self-improvement can change someone from a wicked person into a righteous person."[13]

In the famous Four Questions that we recite as part of the Pesach Haggadah, we ask, if on all other nights we are allowed to eat *chametz* and matzah, why during this time do we eat only matzah? Later in the Haggadah, we're given the answer, "Because the dough of our ancestors did not have time to become leavened before the King of kings, the Holy One, Blessed be He, revealed Himself to them and redeemed them." Here we see that matzah is a form of heavenly bread and that, at this time, we partake from Divine bread at the Holy table, as we relive the story of Exodus; of our redemption from restriction and concealment in Egypt, to revelation and freedom through Hashem's light.

The Forces of Fate

We all know the story of Adam eating from the forbidden fruit of the Tree of Knowledge (*Etz HaDa'at*). The *gematria* (the sum of the numerical value of the letters) of *chametz* and *se'or* (leavening) is 639, the same *gematria* of "*Etz HaDa'at.*" So, on a mystical level, the "fruit" that Adam was restricted from eating was "leavened bread." This was humanity's first taste of godlessness, and the birth of our impaired awareness and evil inclination. Matzah, in contrast, is the *unleavened* bread that symbolizes the perfection and redemption of *da'at*, using our knowledge and awareness to remember and honor that Hashem is everything. As it is written in Likutei Moharan, "we reach Hashem only with intimate knowledge, with experience, with heart and emotion."[14]

During Pesach, we retell the story of Egypt to relive it as if we too are being freed and to remember that we too were once "strangers in a strange land." And though we tell the story of our enslavement, we also remember the importance of not enslaving the stranger, the other, and perhaps most importantly, not becoming enslaved to ourselves (to our illusory identities). As it is written, "Do not hate an Edomite, because he is your brother. Do not hate an Egyptian, because you were a stranger in his land."[15] This verse emphasizes that we should not even hate our enemy, even those that enslaved us, because the only way to be truly free is to be free from hate. As Rabbi Lord Jonathan Sacks says, "If they continued to hate their erstwhile enemies, Moses would have taken the Israelites out of Egypt, but he would not have taken Egypt out of the Israelites. Mentally, they would still be there, slaves to the past. They would still be in chains, not of metal but of the mind—and chains of the mind are the most constricting of all."

The French dramatist Jean Anouilh wrote, "Tragedy is clean, it is restful, it is flawless. In a tragedy, nothing is in doubt and everyone's destiny is known. That makes for tranquility...Tragedy is restful;

and the reason is that hope, that foul, deceitful thing, has no part in it. There isn't any hope." Pesach celebrates the Jews leaving their tragic circumstance in Egypt and the hope that redemption and salvation bring with them into the Promised Land. We end the Haggadah in hope, in prayer, and in unison, with the words, "Next Year in Jerusalem." As Ishay Ribo in his song *Leshuv Habaita* sings, "The time has come to wake up, to leave everything, to overcome, and to return home."[16]

THE PRAYERS OF GRATITUDE

In this *parashah*, we read about the thanksgiving-offering.[17] Thanksgiving signifies awareness, gratitude, action and appreciation, a potent mixture that creates love and redemption. We read that, in the future, all of the sacrifices will be suspended except for the thanksgiving-offering.[18] This is in the time of redemption, when there will be no sin, only thanks to Hashem[19] (as all will be forgiven).[20] Rebbe Nachman speaks of that time, teaching that we will draw ever closer to Hashem, and, as we do, our understanding of Hashem will increase, increasing our desire for thanksgiving in turn. The opposite is true in this time, when we can give thanks to Hashem before the redemption, thereby drawing ourselves closer. As it's written, "All sacrifices will be annulled—but the sacrifice of thanksgiving will not be annulled. All prayers will be annulled, but the prayer of gratitude will not be annulled." As King David sings, "I owe You vows and will offer You thanksgivings."[21] Notice that it's written "thanksgivings" and not "thanksgiving," indicating both the thanksgiving prayer and the prayer of gratitude.

Reb Natan teaches that the thanksgiving-offering symbolizes the union of opposites, as it was brought with both matzah and *chametz*, showing us that we, too, should try and join these opposites together to create true thanksgiving. As we know, on Pesach we eat only matzah, and on Shavuot we bring the thanksgiving loaves (two loaves of bread) as an offering to the *Beit HaMikdash* (Holy Temple). These "opposite" holidays are linked through this *parashah*, which details the thanksgiving-offering and is read before Pesach to remind us that the goal of the Exodus on Pesach was to receive the Torah on Shavuot.[22]

It is Shavuot, which is the 50th day of the count (Omer) from Pesach, that correlates to the 50th Gate of Wisdom. Kabbalistically, the 50th Gate of Wisdom is connected to *Malchut* (Kingship), which, in the Ten Sefirot (Emanations), is the vessel that manifests the Light of *Keter* (Crown). God's Infinite Light originates at a level that is beyond this world, physically inaccessible to us, but it is filtered down through the *Sefirot* until it reaches the *Malchut*, out of which it shines onto us in our finite world.

Rebbe Nachman teaches that the 49 Gates leading up to the 50th gate correspond to the 49 letters that make up the names of the twelve tribes of Israel. Each tribe, therefore, has individual gates for its members, so everyone can return to the Holy One through their own personalized pathway. Shavuot, receiving the Torah, is the 50th and highest Gate, the full *teshuvah*, the complete return to Hashem. Rebbe Nachman always stressed the power of saying *Tehillim* (Psalms) in order to perform *teshuvah*. These 49 days between Pesach and Shavuot are the most powerful time to recite *Tehillim* and return to Hashem. These days leading up to Pesach are a chance for us to get into the mindset of *bitul* (self-nullification), a perspective shift that brings us to thanks, gratitude and a space of *teshuvah*.

As physical creatures, we can't fully defeat the forces of fate, but our souls, the parts of us that are infinite, can connect beyond the finite world. When we choose to burn our *chametz*—the false sustenance of pride and devotion to material gain—and give thanks, we can surpass our limitations and connect to the true and everlasting freedom that can only be found in the Light of the Infinite.

step in rhythm,
grow in concert

When I can't sleep, I often free verse / wax poetic about whatever's on my mind. It's always interesting reading it the next morning. Here's one from the other night:

> *The world*
> *is full*
> *of enough*
> *dissonance*
> *produce*
> *melody*
> *perform*
> *alchemy*
> *sift the good notes*
> *from the bad*
> *the serene*
> *from the siren song*
> *step in rhythm*
> *grow in concert*
> *we are all notes*
> *in this*
> *Divine*
> *or*
> *ch*
> *es*
> *t*
> *ra.*

It seems we all want to be one with our natural state and the spaces we are in—content, fulfilled, thriving. That would seem to be enough, but the truth is we want more than that—we want transcendence. We long to not be bound by the limitations and constrictions of this world; a world where the good is always intertwined with a bit of "bad." Only in the next world is good 100% and bad is nonexistent. When I was a kid, and even today, when I walk out of the theater after seeing a superhero movie, I feel like I have those powers, if only for a little bit. The allure of these comic books turned movies is the thought of breaking free of one's limitations; of ridding oneself of reality, of turning what is natural into supernatural.

In these past *parshiot*, we have been reading about the *mishkan* (the tabernacle) and how Hashem commanded Aharon, the high priest, and his sons to bring special sacrifices for seven days to prepare themselves for their service in the *mishkan*. Every seven days, Moshe would take the *mishkan* apart and put it back together, as the Jews wandered through the desert on their way to the Promised Land. In this week's *parashah*, Shemini, Hebrew for "eight" (referring to the eighth day following the seven days of the inauguration of the Tabernacle), we learn that the service of the *mishkan* actually begins on the eighth day.

As we read, "And it was on the eighth day ... and the glory of the Lord appeared to all the people ... And fire went forth from before the Lord and consumed the burnt offering and the fats upon the altar, and all the people saw, sang praises, and fell upon their faces."[1]

The Kli Yakar, a preeminent medieval Torah scholar, asks why it's called the "eighth day." The Jewish week is seven days, and the consecration of the *Mishkan* was limited to seven days, as it is written, "And you shall not go out of the door of the tent of meeting for seven days, until the days of your consecration be fulfilled, for He shall consecrate you seven days." The Kli Yakar answers his own question, stating that related to the eighth day it is written, "Today the Lord appears to you." Hashem doesn't appear in the *Mishkan* during the seven days of consecration but on and *because* of the eighth day, a day beyond the natural order of things.

Seven is a recurring number in the Torah representing the natural order: seven days of the week; the month of the festivals is Tishrei, the seventh month of the Hebrew calendar; and we have seven-year cycles, culminating in Shemittah (the Sabbatical year). As we learn, seven in Judaism always represents completeness of the natural world, the finite world. So eight, of course, is that one step beyond nature, something more than human, more than finitude—something holy. Shabbat, the seventh day of our week, is a taste of the infinite, but it's still bound in time and space. It's a gift from Hashem that we even get that taste, as it is stated in Talmud Shabbat, "The Holy One, blessed be He, said to Moshe, I have a precious gift in My treasure house, and it is called the Shabbat."[2] The eighth day represents a taste beyond this world.

Eight also brings to mind the ancient ritual of the *brit milah*, circumcision (Avraham's original covenant with God), which happens on the eighth day of a baby boy's life, representing the commitment of his life to something beyond nature, a covenant with Hashem. One can ask, if it is a sign of our covenant with the Holy One, then why would we not be born with it? The answer is because it is our job to take a physical action and create the covenant, a partnership literally seen on the body, that we have taken part in and taken personal action towards. The Arizal teaches that this is part of Adam and Eve's primordial sin and the constant battle we were forced into as humanity, always torn between opposing physical and spiritual inclinations. So much so that it is also the one organ that can bring the potential of the Divine Feminine into creation itself. The *brit milah* acts as a reminder to not get stuck connecting only to our physical impulses and to continue seeking connection to the Infinite.

To emphasize his point of seven being bound by nature in this world and eight representing that which is above nature, in the next world, the Kli Yakar says, (commenting on Talmud Arachim) that the harp that was played in the original sanctuary had seven strings, but the harp that will be played in the Temple of the Messianic Era will have eight strings.[3]

But we can dig even deeper into the Kli Yakar's question and answer. His real question is this: if eight represents unity with God on a *supernatural* level, how can the eighth day have any connection to the seven days prior, which take place purely in the natural world? The phrase "the eighth day" implies a continuation of the previous seven days. So, how do we bridge that gap between the natural and supernatural? How can we move from seven to eight?

The answer that the Lubavitcher Rebbe gives is simple and profound: supernatural revelations depend on human efforts. Hashem designed the world that way. The Messianic age will be brought on only by human's revealing and serving God in *this* world. It is those acts we take in our "seven" days of natural time and space that will bring about the Divine response of the "eighth" day—the infinite—Moshiach. The highest level of holiness is only made possible by our *physical* acts of spirituality. So it is called "the eighth day" not because it naturally follows the seven, but because if we use these seven days to draw close to our Creator, the eighth day becomes the day of *Schechina* (Indwelling Divine presence). The lesson is for us to do all we can in this natural and finite world in order for Hashem to bless our efforts with infinite impact.[4]

The Count-Up

The counting of the Omer is a seven week period—seven weeks of seven days. It is written, "You shall count for yourselves, from the day after the [festival] rest, from the day you bring [before Me] the Omer sacrifice—seven full weeks shall they be. Until the day after these seven full weeks, [Shavuot], shall you count 50 days, and then shall you bring a new offering to Me."[5] Here we see another odd jump in numbers: the Torah commands us to count for 50 days, but it also commands us to count seven weeks, which only adds up to 49 days. But much like "the eighth day" brought on by our seven days of spiritual work in consecrating the Mishkan, the fiftieth day of the Omer is that taste of the Infinite that we get on Shavuot, the holiday that commemorates and recreates our receiving the Torah directly from Hashem at Mount Sinai. That 50th day of high holiness is only made possible by the 49 days of spiritual work that we do in counting the Omer.

As we touched on in the last chapter, Kabbalah teaches that Shavuot, the 50th day of the Omer, correlates to the 50th Gate of Wisdom. Kabbalistically, the 50th Gate of Wisdom is connected to *Malchut* (Kingship), which, in the Ten Sefirot (Emanations), is the vessel that manifests the Light of Keter (Crown). God's Infinite Light originates at a level that is beyond this world, physically inaccessible to us, but it is filtered down through the *Sefirot* until it reaches the *Malchut*, out of which it shines onto us in our finite world.

To understand the significance and the process of these 50 days from Pesach to Shavuot, we need to understand that there are 49 "Gates of Impurity," descending levels of sin, in direct opposition to the 50 Gates of Wisdom. The Kabbalah teaches that, while in Egypt, the Jews descended to the 49th Gate of Impurity. It also took 49 days for our ancestors to travel from Egypt to Mount Sinai, to be prepared to receive God's Divine revelation. Through the counting of the Omer, we have the opportunity to move through our own 49 "Gates of Understanding and Holiness," step by step, day by day.

Rebbe Nachman taught that the 49 Gates correspond to the 49 letters that make up the names of the Twelve Tribes of Israel. Each tribe, therefore, has individual gates for its members, so everyone can return to Hashem through their own personalized pathway. Shavuot, receiving the Torah, is the 50th and highest Gate, the full *teshuvah*, the complete return to Hashem. Rebbe Nachman always stressed the power of saying *Tehillim* (Psalms) in order to perform *teshuvah (a return to Hashem)*. And the 49 days between

Pesach and Shavuot are the most powerful time to recite Tehillim and return to Hashem.

This lesson is reinforced when we learn from the following *pasuk* (verse) related to the Jewish people's exile in Egypt:

וְאֵלֶּה שְׁמוֹת בְּנֵי יִשְׂרָאֵל הַבָּאִים מִצְרָיְמָה אֵת יַעֲקֹב אִישׁ וּבֵיתוֹ בָּאוּ

These are the names of the Children of Israel who went down to Egypt; each man and his wife, they came.[6]

In Hebrew, the last letters of these lines make up the words '*Tehillim*' and '*Teshuvah.*' The verses that follow this one list the names of the tribes (their 49 letters) which correspond to the 49 days of Sefirah which correspond to the 49 Gates of *Teshuvah*.[7] Reb Natan teaches that the daily obstacles we encounter are in direct proportion to the spiritual levels of wisdom we seek to achieve. The 50th gate of understanding is beyond us—it's not something we can achieve ourselves—but, much like "the eight day" and Shabbat, it will come to us as a gift from Hashem by the work that we do within the seven dimensions of space and time in the natural world.

The root of each person's soul has a path. The power of *Tehillim* for the soul is that when one doesn't know how to reach the specific gate of repentance/return, reciting *Tehillim* brings that person's soul to the specific gate of repentance they need to enter.[8] As we learn from Talmud Sotah, "[Man in this world] is like a person traveling in the pitch-dark night... who does not know which path to take."[9] Rabbeinu reminds us, that if you think you are far, remember the words from Devarim,[10] "It is something that is very close to you—in your mouth and your heart, so that you can do it."[11] On the 50th day of the Exodus, "God descended on Mount Sinai."[12] This involved the concept regarding which Hashem said through the last prophet Malachi, "Return to me, and I will return to you."[13] This is the return of the Holy One, the 50th gate of return.

The counting of *Sefirat HaOmer* is meant to prepare us to receive the living Torah anew every Shavuot, and it is our preparation for the 50th Gate, the gate of Wisdom. All of this begins with Pesach, which in *Likutei Halachot* is explained as 'Peh Sach', which means "a talking mouth." This means that the only path to the upper levels of holiness is through speech, through *Tefillah* (prayer), the true speech of calling out to God. We do this by reading *Tehillim* and using speech to speak out and count each day. It's a time when we count and realize that each day is a new beginning, a new opportunity for change, for return, for Oneness, and that each day does indeed count. The blessings you receive correlate to the words that you speak—this is the power of the Omer, of counting out loud with the blessings of *Sefirat HaOmer*.

We cannot reach our ultimate destination in just one holiday. Indeed, Pesach and our Exodus was just the beginning. During the Omer we continue our spiritual ascendance, working to bring ourselves closer to purity, intending to return to Hashem. And it is not until the 50th day—the day beyond the natural—that God returns to us, and we receive the Torah, the ultimate revelation.

In the Absence of the Beit HaMikdash

In the days leading up to Pesach, followed by the days leading up to Shavuot, we read the *parshiot* that detail the *korbanot* (sacrifices), the ways in which we purify ourselves towards transcendence.

With the absence of a *Beit HaMikdash* (Holy Temple) and altar today, it is forbidden to offer sacrifices. However, *chazal* (our sages) tell us that our prayers today are in place of the *korbanot*.[14] In addition to asking Hashem for our needs, prayer is a time to focus on self-improvement. It is a time when we "offer" our animal soul to God, refining our animalistic tendencies and submitting them to Hashem's will.[15] Our most profound sacrifice is when we subdue and harness the overwhelming power of the evil inclination and manage to use that energy for good, for Hashem.

As it's written in this *parashah*—וְהִתְקַדִּשְׁתֶּם וִהְיִיתֶם קְדֹשִׁים—"You are to sanctify yourselves, and you shall become holy."[16] The Chatam Sofer teaches that by using the term וְהִתְקַדִּשְׁתֶּם, the reflexive form of קדשׁ, it's implied that even if one feels they haven't attained any degree of sanctity, they should act as though they are already קדושׁ (holy), and to perform the *mitzvot* that may not even feel aligned in your current spiritual state. By making this initial effort, even though a person may not yet be קדושׁ (holy), וְהִתְקַדִּשְׁתֶּם)), Hashem is assuring us even in this case, that we will ultimately achieve true sanctity (וִהְיִיתֶם קְדֹשִׁים).

As we learn in Talmud Yoma, if one tries to sanctify oneself below, even if just a little bit, the person is helped to be sanctified much more from Above (both in this world and the world to come).[17] "Sanctify a little from below" refers to our *mitzvot* in physicality, while "sanctify much more" from Above refers to the next world tied to the soul. So taking the initial step of וְהִתְקַדִּשְׁתֶּם, acting as קדושׁ, is the stepping stone to attain true קְדֻשָּׁה for holiness's sake or any other sake, which will ultimately lead one to perform the mitzvot for their own sake, leading to sincere קְדֻשָּׁה.

This is a great example of the lesson we learn in Talmud Pesachim, "*Mitoch shelo lishma, bah lishmah,*" which means "even a *mitzvah* performed with ulterior motives garners reward," as Rav Yehuda said that Rav said, "A person should always engage in Torah study and performance of *mitzvot*, even if he does so not for their own sake, as through the performance of *mitzvot* not for their own sake, one gains understanding and comes to perform them for their own sake." The act of giving itself will eventually change the way one feels about giving.[18] As stated before, if our heart compels us to want to hold on and not let go, it is the act of giving and letting go that we must master. And by way of this, we sanctify ourselves and each other.[19] This is when we shift the focus from physicality to spirituality, when our alignment isn't led by the mind, but by the soul.

The biggest takeaway from this *parashah* for me is that when we elevate our soul above our body, aligning our physical selves to our spiritual selves, we can transform our natural space into a supernatural setting.

becoming a
semblance
of God

"The sign of circumcision is, as I think, so important, that I could persuade myself that it alone would preserve the [Jewish] nation forever." —Spinoza

With *parashah* Tazria, we are entering a new section of Vayikra (Leviticus) dealing with the laws of humankind. (The previous *parshiot* dealt with the laws pertaining to animals.) This follows the order of creation: man (*ish*) was created last. Rav Samlai explains that the order is such not because humans were created last, but *for the reason* that humans were created last.

It's simpler to understand the sanctification of the animal world. It's natural for us to make important distinctions between the clean and unclean, *taharah* (purity) and *tumah* (impurity), in the animal world. Humanity's struggles, however, and the work we have to do to sanctify ourselves, is far more complex. The Zohar compares humans to animals regarding the *korban* (sacrifice), deducing from the verse "and the eighth day the skin of the *orlah* should be circumcised"[1] being amidst the verses that deal with *taharah* and *tumah* of the woman giving birth. What we see in these readings in their proximity and importance is the sanctification of time (Shabbat) of human beings, or in this case man, (*brit milah*) and of place (*the korban*). Hashem is *kadosh* (holy) as it says, "for I am Kadosh."[2] We, on the other hand, have the constant struggle to attain *kedushah*. All of this comes to teach us how to free ourselves from our slavery to that which is not holy and to take actions towards holiness, freedom, spirituality and oneness.

If we are all made in the Divine image, but have no actual image of God, then how do we become a semblance of the Infinite Light in the finite that surrounds us? The answer is found in the Alter Rebbe's teaching of the basis and root purpose of the entire Torah—to elevate and exalt the soul high above the body to Hashem, the source and root of all worlds, and to draw down the *Ein Sof* (Infinite

Light). This is done through using the body below to elevate the soul on high.[3]

As we know, Hashem created the world through words—speaking it into existence. Each Hebrew letter composes the building blocks of our reality. The Arizal teaches that within the four letters of Hashem's name, Havayah, (the tetragrammaton, written out as *yud-hei-vav-hei*) the *yud* and *vav* represent aspects of masculinity (*ish*) and the two *hei's* represent aspects of femininity (*ishah*). Kabbalah teaches that the world was created through the letters and energies that compose the four letters of this Divine name. This clearly demonstrates that the male-female dynamic is the spiritual structure that our physical universe depends upon. And since the world and everything in it was composed and is sustained through the name, this dynamic permeates our entire reality.

The ten *sefirot*, Divine channels in which the world was created and are manifested in all aspects of creation, are associated with the four letters of the tetragrammaton. The first *sefirah* that relates to our conscious self, *chochmah* (wisdom), is associated with the first *yud* (י), the masculine, of the Havayah, while the second, *binah* (understanding), is associated with the first *hei* (ה), the upper *hei* (ה), the feminine. The next six emotional *sefirot* are associated with the third letter, the *vav* (ו), the masculine, that also sits between the upper and lower *yud* (ו) in the letter *aleph*. While the tenth *sefirah*, *malchut* (kingdom, sovereignty), is associated with the second or lower *hei* (ה), the feminine.

How Purpose is Sown

In Talmud Sotah, the Gemara describes the battle between David and Goliath. What is implied by the name Goliath? Rabbi Yoḥanan says that the verse indicates that he stood before the Holy One, Blessed be He, with brazenness (*gilui panim*), as it is stated: "Choose yourselves a man (*ish*), and let him come down to me."[4] *Ish* is referring to none other than the Holy One, Blessed be He, as it's written, "The Lord is a man (*ish*) of war."[5] The Holy One, Blessed be He, said, "I will hereby fell him by the son of a man (*ben ish*), as it's written, "Now David was the son of that man (*ben ish*) of Ephrath."[6, 7]

We find the etymological source for the term *ishah* (woman, wife) in the verse, "This one shall be called *ishah*, because this one was taken out of *ish*."[8] Each person and the *sefirot* have masculine and feminine aspects and qualities, The Lubavitcher Rebbe explains that on the level of *ishah* one must occupy oneself with the aspect of *tazria* (sowing). Sowing is specifically done down here on and in the earth, if one were to sow even three spans above the earth, nothing will sprout. It is the same with *mitzvot*, it must be done here on earth. As it's written, "And I will sow her for Me in the earth,"[9] and "For you shall be a land of delight."[10] This is all intended below, not simply in the intellect or emotions, but in actual practice in actual deed.

As we have covered previously, Hashem desires the heart, but it is the heart that must be put into action for elevation to take place. The *mitzvah* of *tzedakah* is the comprehensive principle of all the *mitzvot* and it is not one that can be limited to the heart—the poor can't be sustained with love alone, they need concrete action. Shedding tears for the poor, while not acting and keeping all resources to oneself won't save a life, it is only through the action that we can complete the purpose of creation and our purpose of being created. The Rebbe teaches that this is the meaning of the verse, "A woman that will conceive," because with *ishah* there needs to be *tazria*—sowing on earth below. Reaching exalted levels of the soul is not enough when we are tasked to use the body here on earth elevating it, this is how we bring about the future redemption.[11]

As we jump into this opening *pasuk* (verse), we read about the deeply mystical and mysterious rituals of childbirth and the cleansing of blood impurities. The Torah connects them to one of the most important *mitzvot* in all of Judaism—the *brit milah*, the covenant of circumcision:

וַיְדַבֵּר ה' אֶל־מֹשֶׁה לֵּאמֹר: דַּבֵּר אֶל־בְּנֵי יִשְׂרָאֵל לֵאמֹר אִשָּׁה כִּי תַזְרִיעַ וְיָלְדָה זָכָר וְטָמְאָה שִׁבְעַת יָמִים כִּימֵי נִדַּת דְּוֹתָהּ תִּטְמָא: וּבַיּוֹם הַשְּׁמִינִי יִמּוֹל בְּשַׂר עָרְלָתוֹ.

The Lord spoke to Moses, saying: Speak to the Israelite people thus: When a woman at childbirth bears a male, she shall be unclean seven days; she shall be unclean as at the time of her menstrual infirmity. On the eighth day, the flesh of the boy's foreskin shall be circumcised.[12]

As we covered in the last chapter, the number seven in Judaism always represents completeness of the natural and finite world. The number eight is that one step beyond nature, something more than human, more than finitude—something holy. A boy's circumcision happens on his eighth day, representing the commitment of his life to something beyond nature, a covenant with Hashem. The eighth day represents a taste beyond this world, and it is this ancient ritual that connects a Jewish man to Hashem in an infinite way. Incidentally, having the ritual on the eighth day of the boy's life gives him the opportunity to experience at least one Shabbat prior to his circumcision, preparing him for that moment of transcendence.

Women's parallel covenant to the *brit milah* is to fulfill the laws of *niddah*, the rituals of cleansing connected to the menstrual cycle and childbirth. *Chazal* (our sages) teach that these purity rituals are ultimately a consequence of disobeying Hashem's command not to eat from the Tree of Knowledge of Good and Evil. One of God's punishments for this sin was that Eve, and all women after her, experience the blood of virginal relations and of cyclical menstruation, in addition to the pain and blood loss of childbirth. The Kli Yakar understands this when the Torah says, "She shall become pure from the source of her blood."[13]

The Arizal expounds on this as a part of Adam and Eve's primordial sin and the constant battle we were forced into as humanity, always torn between opposing physical and spiritual inclinations. We are often driven by the one organ that can bring the potential of the Divine Feminine into creation itself or can, God forbid, do the opposite.

Steps Toward the Edenic State

The Gaon of Lutzk explains that when a man wants to enter into the covenant of Avraham, it's done by both *tevilah* in the *mikveh* (ritual bath immersion) and by *brit milah* (circumcision). This is the case when a non-Jew converts to Judaism—he does both rituals himself. When a son is born to a Jewish mother, it is she who goes to the *mikveh*, while the son undergoes the *brit milah*. It is taught that both the mother and male child are spiritually impure in the time following childbirth and have to take action to ascend and become spiritually clean again. The Tzadik of Kotzk says that giving birth lies in the hands of Hashem, which we see in Bereishit: "And Hashem opened her womb"[14] It's said that the *Shechinah*, the Divine Presence, is actually part of the physical process of the child's birth. But when the child is born, the *Shechinah* and her influence depart, and so the mother and child, now at a distance from God, fall into seven days of impurity. Only on the eighth day can either of them become clean again. Eight representing a return to a pure Edenic connection to Hashem.

In essence, *brit milah* is the very first and most fundamental Jewish commandment. In Bereishit, Hashem tells Abraham, "This is My covenant which you shall keep...every male child among you shall be circumcised. And you shall circumcise… and it shall be a token of the covenant."[15] In this sense, *Brit Milah* is the most everlasting, strongest sign of our commitment to God and our heritage.

The Radak's take on circumcision, much like other *mitzvot*, is as a remembrance of our fundamental commitment to Hashem. In the Talmud it says that when King David was naked in a bathhouse, he first thought to himself, "Woe is me, for I stand naked without a single commandment to myself," but then he remembered the circumcision in his flesh and he was comforted.[16]

Brit milah is also obviously the most fundamentally physical of all the commandments. It's performed on the particular organ which is commonly used for sin and lust, which is to teach us an essential tenet of Torah—that out of our darkest physical potential comes the highest spiritual light. This is what distinguishes us from animals. Whereas the animal is stuck in nature and acts only within the laws of reality, our task is to reach beyond nature into the realm of the infinite soul. That is the truest part of our being and why all natural creation preceded our creation. It is precisely *because* we struggle with what we are that we are able to attain the highest possible level of any of Hashem's creations.

On Shabbat morning, we read the *pasuk*, לֹא יִשְׁכְּנוּ עֲרֵלִים, "The uncircumcised shall not abide [in the contentment of Shabbat]." *Chazal* teach that the *brit milah* is on such a high level that even on Shabbat one can perform a *brit milah*, removing the *orlah* (foreskin). It is taught that so long as the infant remains without a brit milah, he is unable to fully absorb the sanctity of Shabbat.[17]

In Sefer Yetzirah, the Kabbalistic *Book of Formation*, it says that the six days of the week are masculine and are six directions pointing outwards. But the Sabbath is feminine, the center point which draws all six points together. Rabbi Aryeh Kaplan says that this teaches us that when we look at ourselves in terms of our external relationships, we are looking at our masculine identity, but when we look at our Self, our inner core, that is a feminine identity. All week long our struggle to gain spirituality is on a male level, but on Shabbat we are on a female level, absorbing the fruits of all that we have done during the week. Without the Sabbath there would be no way of receiving the blessings we create for ourselves. The same relationship is true in biology: the man gives over a million sperm cells, out of which the woman receives only one. She receives a whole multitude of creation, and then gives back completeness. If masculinity is giving, femininity is receiving and completing.[18] We see again the parallel to this week's learning about rituals around childbirth. The Torah is teaching us how essential the sanctification of our sexuality is—it represents the ultimate form and the highest level of emulating the Infinite One by actually perpetuating humanity ourselves. Therefore, it is something that should be treated with the utmost level of spiritual care.

The laws surrounding both birth and circumcision are meant to manifest spiritual transcendence. They keep us from getting stuck connecting only to our physical impulses and remind us to continue seeking connection to the Infinite.

Receive Through Giving

There's a beautiful *chassidic* story that was told at a meal following a *brit milah* celebration. Reb Yitchak Meir of Ger asked one of the *chassidim* present to share a story of Reb Levi Yitzchak of Berditchev. The *chassid* jumped at the chance to share how one of Reb Levi Yitzchak's disciples was a dealer of oxen. At the time, the price for cattle had dropped significantly, which was horrible news for this *chassid*, as he had a lot of cattle at the time and was depending on the sales as a way to provide for his family. Realizing the tremendous financial loss that he was about to incur, he set off for Berditchev to ask his Reb Levi Yitchak for advice and a blessing.

When he arrived, the Rebbe asked him if there was a particular mitzvah that he engaged in that stood out above all others.

He thought to himself, and replied, "Yes, I am a *mohel.*"

The Rebbe replied, "And what do you do if, God forbid, the bleeding doesn't stop after you have circumcised the infant?"

The *mohel*/merchant began to list various medications that he had used in the past.

The Rebbe replied, "I will give you a special herb, so that if, God forbid, you are in a similar predicament, you can apply this herb to the source of the bleeding and, with Hashem's help, it will heal at once."

The merchant took it with pleasure, but still a bit perplexed, looked to the Rebbe and asked, "And what should I do about the cattle business?"

The Rebbe simply looked back at him and said, "But I have already told you—whenever a newly circumcised child bleeds profusely you should apply this herb and with Hashem's help the incision will heal immediately."

So, the merchant set to travel back home.

Reb Yitchak Meir stopped the *chassid* in the midst of telling the story, suggesting, "From this it's clear that the merchant was a *chassid*, since he didn't persist with advice for the cattle business, which had weighed on him the most, instead believing that his Rebbe's words must include an answer to the question that had brought him there, even without understanding how it could possibly be so."

The *chassid* nodded his head and continued with the tale: "On his way home, the merchant stopped at an inn, where he heard that the innkeeper's son was not circumcised. He asked the innkeeper, 'Why have you not yet had your son circumcised?'

The father looked saddened by the inquiry and replied that previously, two of his sons had died as a result of circumcision, because the bleeding could not be stopped. The merchant recalled the words of the *tzaddik* of Berditchev and looked to the innkeeper asking, "What would you give if a solution were to be found for this problem?"

The innkeeper was intrigued and answered, "If it were possible to circumcise my son without danger, I would be prepared to pay four hundred silver rubles."

"I will circumcise him on my responsibility, depositing my own four hundred rubles to be forfeited in case, God forbid, of misfortune," answered the merchant.

The innkeeper, eager to circumcise his son without worry, agreed, provided that the *mohel*/merchant remained with them for four weeks until the child was out of harm's way. The *mohel* went on with the circumcision as promised, and the infant bled heavily, but immediately the *mohel* applied the herb that the *tzadik* had given him and the bleeding stopped immediately.

After a few days, news reached the merchant that the price of oxen had risen again, and he wanted so badly to hurry home to sell his livestock, but the innkeeper held him to his word of staying in the village for the four weeks following the procedure. After a few more days, he heard that the price of livestock had soared even more than before, and he pleaded to be allowed to leave and take care of his other business. But the innkeeper ignored his pleas. Only after the full four weeks had passed did the innkeeper allow the merchant to take leave, but not before paying him both the four hundred silver rubles for the successful brit milah and four hundred rubles that he was holding as collateral.

When the merchant finally returned home, he immediately ran to sell his oxen and found that he could sell them for a far greater amount than he could have imagined, even more than he had heard rumored. He couldn't believe the turn of events and fortune. Right then, he knew he had to travel back to Reb Levi Yitzhak in Berditchev.

Upon his arrival, he greeted the Rebbe and said, "Rebbe, the fee of four hundred rubles belongs to you without a question, and a portion of the profit I made on the sale of my livestock rightly belongs to you as well."[19]

He then understood that all along the Rebbe was telling him, "Tap into the mitzvah that *you* connect with, and if you elevate yourself and your family spiritually through that, your physical wellbeing will be blessed."

One of my favorite lessons from Reb Simcha Bunim is: "Everyone must have two pockets, and a note in each, so that he or she can reach into one or the other, depending on the need. When feeling low and depressed, discouraged or disconsolate, one should reach into the right pocket and there find the words: *Bishvili nivra ha-olam*—"The whole world was created for me."[20] But when feeling high and mighty, one should reach into the left pocket and find the words: *V'anochi afar v'efer*—"I am but dust and ashes."[21]

Kabbalah teaches that the world was created as a broken vessel; Hashem constricted infinity and hid the ultimate good in the brokenness of the world. Reb Natan says that our highest task is to *choose* to see this Infinite Light; to choose to let it in and partner with Hashem. Our laws and customs, in ways so mysterious and in ways very obvious—literally turning our physical bodies into ritual spiritual objects—are the most powerful reminders we have to keep making that choice to strive for something higher. To not let ourselves believe that we are *only* creatures, that we are *only* animals, driven *only* by physical instincts. The Torah teaches us how to free ourselves from our self-imposed slavery; to take actions towards holiness, freedom, and ultimate oneness.

Human beings are but dust of the earth, *Adamah*, but through the struggle and fight to spiritualize reality, we become *Adameh la-Elyon*, a semblance of God.

birds in a trap

Winks from Above

As is customary, in the first 30 days after my mom passed away, my family, friends and I split the responsibility for saying the full Mishnayot, for the purpose of my mom's *aliyat neshama* (soul elevation). When I read mine, I noticed right away that my mom's Hebrew first name was right on top of her Hebrew last name—פרידה צפור—right there in the Mishnah. It was a moment when I felt that she was winking at me, and Hashem was letting me know, "*It's ok, your ima is with you for the rest of your life, as light in infinite recursions.*"

I was reminded of this as I sat down to dive into this week's *parashah*, Metzora. It was a double *parashah* last year, so I am now writing its own *dvar* in completion of this five book series… Again, in the first few *pesukim* (verses), I see not only my mom's name (צפור), but my Hebrew name, (אהרן). It's what we call *hashgacha pratit* (Divine providence), when I see once again not only my mother, her soul and memory in the learning and writing that I'm doing, but her showing me that we are there together; our souls inseparable, our journey in light, infinite.

Staying tapped into *hashgacha pratit*, seeing Divine providence, requires proactive alignment. There is that positive, inspirational, and elevating feeling when one is tapped into one's purpose and connected to one's Creator. Then there is the opposite, when one feels trapped and one's actions feel purposeless; disconnected from service to the Creator and to others. In the *Beit HaMikdash* (Holy Temple), sitting on top of the ark, were the two *keruvim* (winged cherubs). The Talmud teaches us that each of the cherubs had the image of a child's face,[1] and it is written in the Zohar that one was in the likeness of a boy and the other of a girl.[2] When we as a people were in alignment with our Source, the *keruvim* would face each other, but when we were not, they would face away from each other.

Cracking Shells of Darkness

Indeed, the opposing forces manifest as the *yetzer hara* (evil inclination) or *kelipot*. In the world, it's the outer coverings or "shells" that conceal Godly light. In ourselves, it is the negativity or egocentricity that keeps us from connecting to our true selves as creations with a Divine purpose, which connects us to the Divine light. This negativity or ego is like the shell of a fruit; it serves to protect the fruit, just as there are times it is useful for our own self-preservation, but it, too, must be removed to get to the sweetness. We have to remove our layers of ego and negativity to get to the root of our being and purpose.

As we keep learning and needing to remind ourselves, our entire purpose is to reveal the Godly light that is concealed throughout Creation and throughout our beings and experiences. I love how Rav Kook open's his *sefer, Orot Hakodesh*: "The aspiration for the destruction of the world exists in (visible) realities in all its qualities, like there exists aspiration for its building, its elevation and enhancement. The sublime advice of God (i.e. Providence) is to turn from the entrapments of evil, and to elevate man and the world from the depths of evil to the heights of goodness. And for this are man and the world intended; and for this is evil itself also intended, that in the role of a present essential essence, in its inner content, it will also be elevated and be turned to goodness, through its recognizing that the aspiration for evil that is in it is directed to the overall enhancement of goodness."[3]

As we covered in the *How to Exist in Love* chapter, in *parashah,* Tazria, we learned about *tzarot* (sad things), and that tzarot come from *lashon hara* (slander/negative speech), which means one is looking at people and oneself negatively. This ayin hara (evil eye) leads to lashon hara, which means looking at people with a bias towards the left side, the side of *gevurah* (judgment). As we read these *parshiot*, we see the word *nega* (blemish/disease, נֶגַע)

repeated; this is a space which encompasses the lowest form of experience. The Ramban teaches the distinction between *nega* (disease, נגע) and *oneg* (pleasure, ענג) is only in a change of perspective. Hebrew is read from right to left, and in the word *nega* (נגע), you see the ayin (ע) is on the left. And, as the Rebbe Rashab taught the Frierdiker Rebbe, if we lead with *chesed* (loving-kindness), which is when we tap into the right side of the *sefirot* and our own beings, and look through the right eye, so to speak, the ayin (ע) of goodness leads. This is when we can move away from *nega* (נגע) and have *oneg* (pleasure, ענג), which is the highest form of life experience.[4]

Life and Death are Dependent Upon the Tongue

One important principle of manifesting good and subduing the bad is by being protective over one's speech. This *parashah* opens with how to atone for *lashon hara*:

וְצִוָּה הַכֹּהֵן וְלָקַח לַמִּטַּהֵר שְׁתֵּי־צִפֳּרִים חַיּוֹת טְהֹרוֹת וְעֵץ אֶרֶז וּשְׁנִי תוֹלַעַת וְאֵזֹב

The Kohen will command the two live, clean birds, cedar wood, crimson thread and hyssop should be taken for the person undergoing purification.[5]

In the time of the *Beit HaMikdash*, leprosy would befall the person who spoke negatively, as it's stated in the Talmud, "Evil gossip kills three: the one who says it, the one who listens, and the subject of the gossip."[6] And as Otto von Bismarck was quoted saying, "Better pointed bullets than pointed speech."

It's asked why must the person bring two birds to sacrifice? *Chazal* (our sages) teach, "Let the chattering birds come and effect forgiveness for the chattering person."[7]

We all want a *shem tov* (good name). People spend their lives trying to protect their reputation. When a person's reputation takes a hit, especially when it is baseless, they feel powerless, and often afraid and ashamed. '*Tiu lien*' in Chinese means 'lose face' because that is the feeling of the person whose reputation has been tarnished; they feel unable to show their face in public, or, in a more extreme circumstance, as if they no longer exist the way they once did. As it's written in Mishlei, "Life and death are dependent on the tongue (speech)."[8]

The Talmud teaches that "just as the learning of Torah equals all other *mitzvot* combined, so does speaking *lashon hara* equal all sins combined." The Chofetz Chayim, who wrote two books on *lashon hara*—*Sefer Chofetz Chaim* and *Sefer Shmiras Halashon*— teaches that *sinat chinam* (baseless hatred) is equal to idol worship, immorality and murder. This is what the Gemara says regarding *lashon hara*: "For three sins a person is punished in this world and has no share in the World to Come: idol worship, immorality, and murder—and *lashon hara* equals them all."[9]

Jumping back to the lesson from the Talmud of the three people killed, it's interesting to note that from there we learn that the person who is damaged most of all is not the one who is gossiping but the one who is listening to the gossip. The reason being that the listener is the one who has the power to stop the *lashon hara*. The person speaking has already decided to gossip, and the subject of the *lashon hara* is not physically present. Only the listener can change the negative speech into something positive or stop it all together, and so the onus is on them.

The Chofetz Chaim teaches that Hashem, in His infinite wisdom, has decreed that *satan*'s (the *sitra achra*'s) power to accuse us is directly related to how we speak about one another. When we refrain from speaking badly about one another, then God, like a loving parent, is willing to overlook our misdeeds. However, when we accuse one another of wrongdoing through *lashon hara*, we give *satan* power to stand before Hashem and accuse us of wrongdoing.

There's a book by Lori Palatnik and Bob Burg titled, *Gossip – Ten Pathways to Eliminate It From Your Life and Transform Your Soul*, and in it, they break down the Ten Pathways of Positive Speech:

1. Speak No Evil – Say only positive statements. Let words of kindness be on your tongue.
2. Hear No Evil – Refuse to listen to gossip, slander and other negative forms of speech.
3. Don't Rationalize Destructive Speech – Excuses like "But it's true" or "I'm only joking" or "I can tell my spouse anything" just don't cut it.
4. See No Evil – Judge people favorably, the way you would want them to judge you.
5. Beware of Speaking Evil Without Saying an Evil Word – Body language and even positive speech can bring tremendous destruction.
6. Be Humble; Avoid Arrogance – These will be your greatest weapons against destructive speech.
7. Beware of Repeating Information – "Loose lips sink ships." Even positive information needs permission before being repeated.
8. Honesty Really Is the Best Policy – Most of the time. Be careful to always tell the truth, unless it will hurt others, break your own privacy or publicize your accomplishments.
9. Learn to Say "I'm Sorry" – Everyone makes mistakes. If you've spoken badly about someone, clear it up immediately.
10. Forgive – If you have been wronged, let it go.[10]

Almost a thousand years earlier, as reported by the Ben Ish Chai, Rambam, in his *perush* (explanation) of the *Mishnayot*,[11] divided speech into five categories:

1. מצוה בו – (Has a *mitzvah* within it), which deals with Torah learning, *tefilot*, and reciting grace and gratitude to Hashem.
2. אהוב – (Beloved), which is about the good and superior intellectual qualities of a person.
3. מתר – (Allowed), which covers speech that is used on a daily basis for negotiations and to conduct business transactions.
4. נזהר ממנו – (Be careful about it), which covers speech which includes lies, flattery (or hypocrisy), gossip (or slander), clowning and other forms of *lashon hara*.
5. נמאס – (Disgusting), which covers "שיחה בטלה" "useless or idle speech."[12]

There is a Midrash that tells the story of a peddler who proclaimed, "Who wants life? Who wants life?" Rabbi Yannai approached the peddler, curious as to what elixir he might be peddling that could guarantee long life. The peddler looked at Rabbi Yannai and simply said that neither he nor any *talmid chacham* would require such an elixir.[13] As others inquired, the peddler took out a book of *Tehillim* pointing to the *pasuk:*

מִי־הָאִישׁ הֶחָפֵץ חַיִּים...נְצֹר לְשׁוֹנְךָ מֵרָע

Which man desires life?... Guard your tongue from evil.[14]

The Antidote of Song

Rebbe Nachman teaches in *Likutey Moharan* that when someone listens to the singing of someone who is wicked, it's detrimental to one's connection to the Creator. But listening to a singer who is virtuous, helps one to connect. Rabbeinu explains that the reason is that the voice is drawn from the birds.[15] Kabbalistically, the two birds in our *pasuk* represent *zeir anpin* and *malchut*, which correspond to the voice and speech. The two birds also represent the two *keruvim*, (cherubs) on the ark that were the source of prophecy in the *Beit HaMikdash* (Holy Temple). It's written in the *Zohar* that these two birds nurse from the same place that prophets nurse.[16] Rabbeinu explains that this is why a singer is called *ChaZaN* (חזן, singer/cantor), from the word *ChaZoN* (חזון, vision), which connotes prophecy, as we see throughout scripture (e.g. "The chazon of Yeshayahu...").[17] This is to say that the *chazan* takes their song from the same place that the prophets take their prophecy.

Kabbalists explain that music helps banish extraneous thoughts and clear the mind, cutting away impure thoughts (*kelipot*) that envelop the soul, allowing a person to connect to the Light of the Infinite. Music is also something that can be played in circles infinitely. In fact that is often how the prophets would reach their state of *nevuah* (prophecy). There would be a repetitive riff being played until it would start to act as a mantra, a meditation, and then prophecy would be reached. As it's written, "a group of prophets... preceded by a lyre, a timbrel, a flute, and a harp; and then will be prophesying,"[18] and "As the musician played, God's Hand came upon him..."[19]

Within us all is the power for *kedushah* (holiness) and/or the power of the *sitra achra* (the opposing forces). Rabbeinu teaches that when a singer is wicked, they take their song from the other birds, from the *kelipot* (evil forces), as it's written in the Zohar that the birds of *kelipah* nurse from the breasts of *Malchut* (Kingship).[20] And when *chatzot* (midnight) comes, a cry goes out, as it's written in *Ecclesiastes*, "As birds are caught in a trap, so too are men caught/ensnared."[21] This alludes to our becoming trapped in the *sitra achra*, while "birds" alludes to the two birds of the *kelipah* that become caught in the trap at midnight. The birds, when aligned like the *keruvim*, are that of *kedushah*, but when they are not aligned and are tied to the *kelipah*, to the *sitra achra*, they are like the *keruvim* facing opposite ways, drawing nourishment from the *kelipot*. And it is that source of nourishment that causes the entrapment fueled by the opposite of *kedushah*. However, through the song within ourselves that is holy, the *malchut* of holiness is uplifted and elevated so that Hashem's light is revealed in this world.

Singing in the Dark

At night, one can be drawn to their *yetzer hara* and busy themselves with desires that take them further away from being connected to the Light of the Infinite. As it's written in the Zohar, "When the night is split (i.e. at midnight), then a call goes out, 'Like birds caught in a trap, so too are men caught.'" But on the other end, there is an opportunity in the darkness to connect on a deeper level, to wake up from one's spiritual slumber.

The Zohar and Rebbe Nachman stress the importance of *Tikkun Chatzot* (Midnight Lamentations), which is also the time that King David would play his harp and compose his psalms. It is this act of lamentations that shifts sleep and dreams from a place of Freudian, *yetzer hara* desires, to an elevated space of rejuvenation and connection. King David said, "At midnight, I will rise..."[22] as he wrote, "Awake, my glory; awake O harp and lyre! I will awaken the dawn."[23]

Rebbe Nachman expands on *ruach* and rhythm in possibly his most famous and fundamental teaching from Likutey Moharan, Reish Pei Bet (282), also known as *"Azamra"* ('I will sing'). Rabbeinu teaches that judging everyone and yourself favorably, always looking for the good points, is essentially the secret to blessings and happiness. It also ensures switching from a frame of mind of *din* (judgment) and speaking *lashon hara,* to one of seeing the good and speaking only positively. Rabbeinu explains that sifting the good from the bad is how melodies are made. We see this through playing a musical instrument, which gathers the good *ruach* from the *ruach* of gloom/depression. In essence, music is made through the separation of good from evil, by selecting and gathering the good points and good notes from the bad; that is how beautiful songs are created. So when a person doesn't let themselves fall, but revives themselves by searching and seeking out the good points in their inner world and in others, gathering and separating those good points from evil and impurity within, this is how melodies of harmony manifest; this is how we are able pray, sing, and give praise to Hashem in *teshuvah* (a return and a repentance), which brings life, happiness and ultimate unification.[24]

Rabbi Aharon Kotler reminds us that to be unified and wholehearted with the Holy One means not to live a life of contradictions, and that someone who speaks *lashon hara* lives a life of contradictions. It's not easy, as it is something that often comes naturally—sharing a story or an experience involving another person—but the more we are careful to only uplift each other through speech (especially when the person isn't present) and deed, the more we are aligned with positivity and light. This incredible pianist asked me yesterday what I think the purpose of life is, and I said that it's to reveal Hashem's light in this world; to reveal what is concealed. And that is how we shine our own light, which brings forth everyone's light, which is the only way for us to bring awareness to the light of the infinite and usher in the final redemption.

G.O.A.T.
amongst
goats

"I visualize what it is, not what it isn't." —Nas

The first *pasuk* (verse) of this week's *parashah*, Acharei Mot, reads:

וַיְדַבֵּר ה' אֶל־מֹשֶׁה אַחֲרֵי מוֹת שְׁנֵי בְּנֵי אַהֲרֹן בְּקָרְבָתָם לִפְנֵי־ה' וַיָּמֻתוּ

Hashem spoke to Moshe after the death of Aharon's two sons [Nadav and Avihu], who drew close to Hashem and died.[1]

Or HaChayim explains that the sins of Nadav and Avihu were very different from sins as we generally understand them. He explains that their sin involved allowing themselves to cling to Hashem so totally that their souls simply left their bodies. It's written "who drew close to Hashem and died" because it was the drawing close that caused their deaths.[2]

We are tasked with reaching towards *hispashtut hagashmiyut*, divesting oneself of materiality.[3] But this spiritual ascent must be balanced. There is the concept of *ratzo ve'shov*, which means to run and to return. That *ratzo* must always be coupled with *shov*. *Ratzo* being the state of *dveykut* (longing to cleave to Hashem), the insatiable desire of the *neshama* (soul) to transcend its material existence, to "run forward" and cling and cleave to its Source. *Shov* is the *neshama's* awakening and determination to "return" and fulfill its mission, using the body, making the physical world a dwelling place for God. This explains *chazal's* statement, "Against your will, you live."[4] As much as our souls yearn to leave our bodies, it is our mission to fulfill the task that can only be done when the soul utilizes and elevates the body. Nadav and Avihu's sin was abandoning the *shov*, the mission of this world. The Lubavitcher Rebbe explains that their yearning was not balanced with a commitment to worldly service[5].

We might not have the same struggle on the level of worrying about our souls ascending so high that they don't return to the body, but in our own world, we need to balance our spiritual and material pursuits. As it's stated in the Talmud, just as we are amply rewarded for performing *avodat* (in service of) Hashem, so too, at times we are rewarded for refraining—if what we're looking to attain is beyond our spiritual grasp.[6] As we can all feel, everything, especially wellness, is about balance. But how do we find balance? How do we control our thoughts, lessen our anxiety and become more present...? Anxiety is born of worry of what might be. Faith is trusting the process and future while focusing on the moment.

The Gift of Being Present

I post photos of moments when I'm elated being around my kids and watching how much of life they are loving. It's almost ironic snapping a photo because it breaks the moment for a second, but I want to capture them and these priceless memories. Often I'll post them later to my social media with the caption, "Life can be so precious, when you're present." Even taking a photo can be a way of being present, not just appreciating a moment but taking action inspired by how in it we really are. So many other moments we are present in the body, but the mind is somewhere else. Balance is about being present. When we start to drift to the future or past or the "what ifs" and "shouldn't haves," that breeds anxiety and takes away from enjoying the short amount of time we are gifted in this world to find and create our purpose, and to shine and share light and love.

Easier said than done. Anxiety is so prevalent throughout humanity and rears its ugly head in so many different ways, crippling in more extreme circumstances. In those moments, it seems we all share a sort of long term memory loss—that actually we have gotten through to the other side, each time. Our mantra should be that things will continue to work out, as they always have.

Because if things are bitter in the moment or might turn sour in the near future, what is often followed down the line is an epiphany and the clarity of why it wasn't for you. That's why the saying 'hindsight is 20/20' is so popular, because when we are uncertain and faithless, we can't see what's meant for us with any sort of clarity—we are far from 20/20 when in that space. But as time passes, we often clearly see that everything played out as it was meant to. The saying means: It's easier to analyze and evaluate situations clearly when we're looking back on them in the past than when we're in the present moment.

Last week, we read about the two birds in the purification of *metzora* atoning for *lashon hara* (negative speech). One is for *taharah* (purity) and the other is sent away. This week in *parashah* Acharei Mot, we read about the *se-irim* (translated as goats, hairy male goats, goat-demons, or in this case scapegoats) for Yom Kippur. One is for Hashem and the second for *Azazel*. This happens after the *Kohen Gadol* (high priest) bathes and puts on sacred linen garments, as it's written:

וְלָקַח אֶת־שְׁנֵי הַשְּׂעִירִם וְהֶעֱמִיד אֹתָם לִפְנֵי ה' פֶּתַח אֹהֶל מוֹעֵד. וְנָתַן אַהֲרֹן עַל־שְׁנֵי הַשְּׂעִירִם גֹּרָלוֹת גּוֹרָל אֶחָד לַה' וְגוֹרָל אֶחָד לַעֲזָאזֵל. וְהִקְרִיב אַהֲרֹן אֶת־הַשָּׂעִיר אֲשֶׁר עָלָה עָלָיו הַגּוֹרָל לַה' וְעָשָׂהוּ חַטָּאת. וְהַשָּׂעִיר אֲשֶׁר עָלָה עָלָיו הַגּוֹרָל לַעֲזָאזֵל יָעֳמַד־חַי לִפְנֵי ה' לְכַפֵּר

Then he shall take the two se-irim and stand them in front of God at the entrance of the Tent of Meeting. And Aaron shall place lots on the two se-irim: one lot for God and one lot for Azazel. Then Aaron shall bring forward the sa-ir for which the lot for God came up, and he shall make it the reparation-offering. And the sa-ir for which the lot for Azazel came up, it shall stand alive in front of God, to make atonement upon it. And he shall send it to Azazel in the wilderness.[7]

As we read, one of the *se'irim* would be elevated as a holy sacrifice and the other sent to the desert to die. Sforno explains that the one that carries all the sins of B'nei Yisrael is not fit to be sacrificed because of the amount of *tumah* (impurity) it carries. In a general sense or what is looked at as karma, punishment is the consequence of sin, as is stated in Yirmiyahu, "Your own wickedness will punish you."[8] That is if actions in *teshuvah* (return, repentance) and actions in *taharah* are not taken. The *se'irim* serve two purposes, one is to transfer the impurities of the person to the animal which releases the person from the punishment that karma brings. The *sa'ir* (goat) that is sacrificed in the *Beit HaMikdash* atones for deliberate sins related to the *Beit Hamikdash*, but the *sa'ir* for *Azazel* (also called the *goral*, the lot that is cast) carries with it the rest of the sins of *B'nei Yisrael*.

As it's written:

> *And Aaron shall lay both his hands on the head of the living sa-ir, and he shall confess over it all the crimes of the Israelites and all their transgressions for all their wrongdoing, and he shall place them on the head of the sa-ir, and send it by the hand of a designated man into the wilderness. Then the sa-ir will carry off all the crimes on itself to a cut-off land; he shall send out the sa-ir into the wilderness.*[9]

Some commentators point to the similarity in name and the allusions to Mount Seir, the home of Esav and the *sair*. The bird last week and the *sair* in this week's *parashah* that are sent away as a sort of gift to the forces of *tumah* (impurity), which are personified by Esav and his שׂר (*sar*)—the angel associated with him. The Abarbanel teaches that the two *se'irim* symbolize the eternal struggle between Yaakov and Esav.

All the stories of the Torah are actually the stories in our own lives as well. We are all microcosms of the universe, these stories playing out inside of us, just as we play out life as a story in the expanse of reality. We all have Esav and Yaakov in us, their struggle is our own. We need to defeat the parts that are Esav's within us all, and the two birds and the two goats are manifestations of both this struggle and steps towards its rectification and elevation.

We learn in the Talmud that the *mitzvah* is to take two goats that are similar in age, height and appearance.[10] Reb Natan teaches that regardless of their being almost identical, one is dedicated to Hashem and the other to Azazel. And in a similar fashion, falsehood and truth can sometimes seem identical, being hard to differentiate. *Se'IRim* (שעירים) represents *Sei'AR* (hair, שער), reminding us that a hairsbreadth is all that separates between holiness and its opposite.[11] And in the same way we relied on Hashem for which goat was for holiness and which for the *sitra achra* (the other side), we need to pray for the same clarity for Hashem to show us the difference between falsehood and truth.[12]

Everything in this world has the power for good or for evil, for elevation or degradation, just as we read about with the two goats. Even with air and breathing there is *kedushah* and *sitra achra*, Rebbe Nachman teaches that there are two "lifelines" that we can draw in when breathing in air, one is the lifeline of *kedusha*, the other is of *tumah*. The righteous draw in pure air, while the evil draw in impure air. To survive, we need to draw air from one of these two channels. When a person regrets their misdeeds and decides to do *teshuvah*, they sever their link with the impure source of air and begin to breathe fresh, new air from the source of holiness.[13] As we learn in Talmud Yuma, "When one repents out of love, his sins become like merits."[14]

So much of staying grounded in truth and being balanced is letting go of all the cacophony that surrounds and tries to distort being truly present in the experiences and moments we find ourselves in. The power of *niggunim* (melodies), when sung in a group of people, is that when we use our breath to connect making music with the instrument that sustains us (our breath/voice), we connect to our essence and the essence of those around us. It's a moment when we shift from thinking or over thinking, to letting go of the extraneous and bringing our breath outward to awaken our soul, we tend to lose ourselves while inspiring ourselves at the same time.

I'll leave you off with what feels like a mantra to me, it's Pharrell on his song, "ESP":

> *Detach yourself (let go, let go, let go, let go, let go)*
> *Re-pack yourself*
> *Be back yourself (let go, let go, let go, let go, let go)*
> *And dream as yourself*
> *Be seen as yourself (let go, let go, let go, let go, let go)*
> *Beam as yourself*
> *Scream as yourself (let go, let go, let go, let go, let go)*
> *And be king of yourself*[15]

cheat codes
to holiness

"My kedushah (holiness) is greater than yours."

—The Maggid of Mezrich

People always tell me it's "so LA" to talk about energy and vibes, but I think perhaps it's just more openly discussed here. In truth, we all feel and are affected by both. That's why it's so important to be mindful of the company we keep. I often place myself in what I call sacred spaces or spiritual environments because when people are there to reach higher levels of being, it means the base level of what's expected is generally pretty elevated. I often go to spaces that one Rabbi in particular will be at, and people ask if I am a *chassid* of his. I'm not, but I find it inspiring to be in the presence of both this Rebbe and the people that do follow him.

I try to catch *Mishmar*, which all over the world tends to be a Thursday night tradition for enrichment and spiritual growth. *Mishmar* in Hebrew means "guard." It's named *Mishmar* because, similar to a military rotation of a watch, a community encourages people and often appoints a leader or speaker to keep the spiritual life going. The last one I attended was at the beautiful, artful, and very LA-styled house of Yitzy Katz. David Sacks spoke, and I don't believe I have ever heard him speak without being completely blown away by his stories, his fresh perspective and his delivery. He's always sure to not go even one minute over, and so we went from the outside area into the dining room, all crowded, feeling as if we were in Jerusalem or Bnei Brak, packed in as tight as can be, so that we could be close to the Rebbe. But in this case, it was in order to be close to creating holiness. Just then one of the guys began singing a *niggun* (chassidic, devotional melody) and everyone joined in. It was as if we were all melding into one, and our individual worries began to wash away. We then got more lively and the energy elevated. I remember just then, I turned to my friend Shua and said, "This is dope, this is what I needed right now." And he replied, "This is why I come every time; it grounds me during the week. Singing in this space reminds me that everything I'm worried about is small and will be fine, and this connects me to what matters and reminds me of why we're alive." I felt the holiness of each one of us raising each other up.

Kedoshim ("holy ones") is my Bar Mitzvah *parashah*. I always considered myself lucky, because it was a short one, and I had to memorize the trope to get all the notes and nuances correct. So, with it being slightly less of a daunting task because of its length, I was able to sing it to everyone present without any mistakes.

The Abarbanel teaches that the *parashah* of Kedoshim repeats all the *mitzvot* mentioned previously to stress that they are meant to be practiced in an atmosphere of *kedushah* (holiness) and not ever to be practiced mindlessly as a habit. We demonstrate this when we perform a *mitzvah* saying,

אֲשֶׁר קִדְּשָׁנוּ בְּמִצְוֹתָיו

"Who has made us holy with His mitzvot."

We proclaim that the *mitzvot* are the basis for *kedushah* and, as our sages say, "Whoever sanctifies himself from below is sanctified from above."[1] The recurring theme throughout all these *dvars* I write is how to bring more blessings into our lives. It started with my project "Don't Block Your Blessings." And now, looking at the weekly Torah readings and Kabbalah with this project, "Light of Infinite," I'm hoping these words inspire you to delve deeper into the Torah and kabbalistic texts, and, as Chaim Vital says, "One can go deeper and deeper, as far as the human mind can delve, and it will always yield new treasures."

As I often say, life can be so precious if you are truly present, and the Torah is the present that presents the tools of how to sanctify time, space, and oneself. When we have full faith that "this world is like a corridor to the World to Come,"[2] we can tap more into our purpose and our spirit and worry less about the temporal "realities" of this material world. Abraham Joshua Heschel writes in *Man in Search of God*: religion begins with a consciousness that something is asked of us. It is in that tense, eternal asking in which the soul is caught and in which man's answer is elicited.[3]

This in a sense was what Munbaz, a righteous king who lived at the end of the Second *Beit HaMikdash* (Holy Temple) era, meant when he answered his detractors stating, "My ancestors stored for this world, but I stored for the World to Come." King Munbaz was a convert, the son of Queen Heleni. During a famine Munbaz opened the royal treasures and disbursed the riches to the poor. His family, angry at the loss of their wealth, united against him: "How can you do this? Your ancestors gathered and saved treasures only ever adding to them, and you squandered it all!" He explained that they stored money, he stored souls. They stored the riches only for themselves while he shared the riches with the poor and united souls, the ultimate in *ahavat Yisrael* (love of one another and Israel). And in an attempt to explain in a way that they might understand, he said he was storing the ultimate reward, the reward in the World to Come.

Holy Curiosities

Albert Einstein was quoted in *LIFE* magazine in conversation with William Miller sharing, "The important thing is not to stop questioning; curiosity has its own reason for existing. One cannot help but be in awe when contemplating the mysteries of eternity, of life, of the marvelous structure of reality. It is enough if one tries merely to comprehend a little of the mystery every day. The important thing is not to stop questioning; never lose a holy curiosity.[4]"

The *parashah* opens commanding us to be holy, קְדֹשִׁים תִּהְיוּ ("Be Holy [because, I, God your Lord am holy]"),[5] implying that we should always seek greater levels of *kedushah*. We can also interpret the Hebrew words קְדֹשִׁים תִּהְיוּ as a Divine assurance that we *will* attain *kedushah*, if we sanctify Hashem's name. As we learn in Pirkei Avot,[6] "One who honors Torah, will be honored…."[7]

As we read further in the *parashah*, "Observe My Sabbaths and fear My Sanctuary; I am God."[8] Reb Natan teaches that the main tool a person can use to subdue materialism and elevate their spirituality is awe and fear of Hashem, explaining that "Fear My Sanctuary" means that if one has fear, they can experience "My Temple [for they have ascended above materialism]."[9]

When the Maggid said, *"My kedushah (holiness) is greater than yours,"* he wasn't saying "I'm holier than you are," rather that "My kedushah *stems* from your kedushah." This connects to a fundamental Torah concept, מצווה גוררת מצווה (*mitzvah goreret mitzvah*), which means that one good deed always pulls another one in its wake. The Maggid takes this idea into the realm of *kedushah*: if someone else does a holy act, it inspires you to be holier for yourself and for others, and so your holiness increases beyond the initial act. So, the Maggid is saying that your *kedushah* makes his *kedushah* greater because each of us has the power to make others holier. And as Abraham Joshua Heschel reminds us, 'Every Moment Is an Opportunity for Greatness.'

One cheat code to heaven is that of the *mitzvot* and teaching Torah to others. The Lubavitcher Rebbe teaches that by bringing another close to the Torah, one becomes their teacher, and the disciple will argue in *Olam Habah* (the World to Come), "I cannot be here without my master."[10] And so the one who shared Torah will be immediately placed in *Gan Eden*.[11]

Rashi points out that this *parashah* "must be read in a public assembly," שרוב גופי תורה תלויין בה,[12] because the holiness of the Torah has no place in isolation. The fundamental purpose of Torah is to teach us to love our fellow humans and bring them closer to *kedushah*. And the midrash says, "If you make yourself holy, I will consider it as if you made Me holy." If we limit our pursuits to nature, Hashem acts naturally towards us; if we raise ourselves above nature, Hashem's dealings with us are supernatural.

My Soul Clings to You

But faced with this daunting task of making ourselves and even Hashem holy, the Oheiv Yisrael teaches that one might say, "How can we attain that level, since our lusts control our desires? How is it possible that when one engages in physical pleasures he adds to the dimensions of *perishah* (separateness) and *kedushah*?" It is for this reason that the Torah states this week:

כִּי קָדוֹשׁ אֲנִי יְהֹוָה אֱלֹהֵיכָם

"For I, Hashem, your G-d, am holy."[13]

Just as Hashem fills all the worlds and beyond but is separate from it, we too must exist in this world, interface with physicality and humanity, without becoming engulfed by it. We are made in Hashem's image, so our purpose is to try to emulate His holy presence in the world and His holy transcendence of it.

The Chatam Sofer points out that the two distinct names of Hashem used in this phrase, כִּי קָדוֹשׁ אֲנִי יְהֹוָה אֱלֹהֵיכָם, come to teach us two different ways God relates to the world and that we can relate to God. The first, ה', is the Name that is totally beyond our comprehension. But it is followed by, אֱלֹהֵיכָם, literally "*our* God", which implies the special and intimate relationship between us and the

Infinite One. Even the preceding words, קָדוֹשׁ אֲנִי, "I am holy," imply this dual relationship. While קָדוֹשׁ (kadosh) implies separation from this world, the preceding word of אֲנִי, "I", is there to imply Hashem's personal closeness to us. So, being made in Hashem's image, we must separate ourselves from the world in ways, abstain from certain materialism, but also make ourselves close to the world, elevating the mundane, spiritualizing reality[14].

Hashem called to Moshe from the mountain, saying, "...if you hearken well to Me and observe My covenant, you shall be to Me the most beloved treasure of all peoples, for Mine is the entire world. You shall be to me a kingdom of priests and a holy nation.' These are the words you shall speak to the children of Israel."[15] Our task is to be a "kingdom of priests and a holy nation." This "priestly function" is manifested through being *kadosh*, fulfilling the *mitzvot* in our private lives, and so bringing God-consciousness and holiness to the world. We bring Hashem to the world and the world closer to Hashem. The prophet Isaiah termed the "priestly function" as a "light to the nations",[16] which is to sanctify oneself and uplift those around you, not to separate and isolate oneself.

The Alter Rebbe points to Proverbs, "The soul of man is a lamp of God,"[17] teaching that just like the flame of the lamp strains upwards, seeking to tear free of the wick and rise heavenward; so, too, does the Godly soul in each of us constantly strive to tear free of the body and material existence, and be nullified within its source in God. And as the Ramchal stresses in *Mesilat Yesharim*, even when one is engaged in the physical activities required by the body, the soul must not deviate from its elevated intimacy, as is stated, "My soul clings to You; Your right arm sustains me."[18] If one sanctifies himself with the Holiness of his Creator even his physical actions come to partake of holiness.[19] The Chatam Sofer points towards Avraham Avinu as a role model in this regard, that despite his exalted status, he not only invited in his contemporaries, he had a great impact on them. And it was because of this aspect of his *kedushah*—being concerned about the spiritual welfare of others—that he was elevated and was a manifestation of קְדֹשִׁים תִּהְיֶה.

As the famous dictum goes, "Who is wise? The person who learns from everyone."[20] This means that everyone has something that another person can learn from them. And so everyone is a "rich person" in this regard by virtue of their unique quality. And as it's written in Likkutei Sichot, it follows then that everyone is obligated to use their unique quality and talent to benefit others who do not possess it, and from this that person will be blessed from Above with those things which they may not possess. As we know from the first time blessings were written in the Torah, it's stated, "those who bless, shall be blessed."[21] It is even more important to follow this path, because the converse is also true, as it's stated explicitly in the Gemara, "when failing to benefit another, there will be a lack in blessings and help from Above." The Gemara concludes stating that the rich themselves may become poor.[22]

The Lubavitcher Rebbe relates that Torah without *ahavat Yisrael* will cease in the end. Relating a story of Levi Yitzchak of Berdichev's hearing three teachings from the Baal Shem Tov, one of them pertained exactly to this.[23] The Baal Shem stressed that "All Torah that is not combined with work will ultimately cease."[24] The term 'work' refers to effort in *Ahavat Yisrael*. Essentially, if the Torah is to continue to endure, it must be combined with effort in *ahavat Yisrael*. The lesson had such a profound impact on Reb Levi Yitzchak that all his life was devoted to efforts on behalf of *ahavat Yisrael*[25].

The great Rabbi Akiva taught that the fundamental principle of the Torah is the commandment which we read this week—to 'Love your neighbor as yourself.'[26] Many ask if that is possible, when our default is selfishness and making sure first and foremost that we are taken care of. The Baal Shem Tov expounds on Rabbi Akiva's lesson that, though we are aware of our many faults, we still look out for and love ourselves, and we need to do the same for those around us despite their faults. This is why these commandments to be holy were given in public assembly, as 'my holiness is your holiness' and vice versa—we need to uplift and elevate and that could only be done when leading with love of the "neighbor as yourself."

The Heights of Holy Sexuality

If we look at the *mitzvot* connected to childbirth and sex and compare them to other traditions' views and practices, the differences are significant. In some other religions, the clergy, the holiest practitioners of those religions, have to remain unmarried in order to avoid any sexual thought or behavior; holiness is synonymous with abstention. In Judaism, sex is considered one of the most holy acts we can partake in, as it is a way in which we become partners with Hashem in creating. Just as we are meant to live in the world in all other ways with holy intentions, we are tasked with having sex with holy intentions and in a way of holiness, so as to elevate something that has the potential for the great darkness into infinite light.

As Rabbi Moshe Yaakov Wisnefsky writes in his preface to his translation of The Arizal's Divrei Torah:

> *We see in these teachings the awesome power of the misuse of sexual energy as well as the sublime heights to which holy sexuality can lift us. Yes, it is easier to follow the extreme of total denial or the extreme of total indulgence; it is far more challenging to take the middle path and fuse intense physicality and intense spirituality. But the rewards of taking the latter path are far greater, and it is really the only way to navigate the pitfalls endemic to the extremes. God has programmed us with both a strong sexual drive and a*

strong spiritual drive, and ignoring one at the expense of
the other is simply a recipe for disaster[27].

The Arizal explains this is all part of Adam and Eve's primordial sin and the constant battle we were forced into as humanity, always torn between opposing physical and spiritual inclinations. The more we act in a way of holiness, the more our spiritual inclinations connect us to Hashem. Through our partnership with Hashem, choosing right over wrong, elevation over desecration, we grow spiritually, and then the spiritual everlasting rewards come. As we covered a few chapters ago, The Zohar compares man to animals in regards to the *korban*, deducing from the verse "and the eighth day the skin of the *orlah* should be circumcised" being amidst the verses that deal with *tumah* (impurity) and *taharah* (purity) of the woman giving birth. What we see in these readings, in both proximity and importance, is the sanctification of time (Shabbat) of man (*brit milah*) and of place (the *korban*). Hashem is *kadosh* as it says, "for I am Kadosh.[28]" We, on the other hand, have the constant struggle to attain *kedushah*. All of this comes to teach us how to free ourselves from that which is not holy and to take actions towards holiness, freedom, spirituality and oneness. But all of this can't be done in isolation; it must be done by inspiring each other, being lights for each other, and by virtue of that, ourselves.

Rabbi Shlomo Ganzfried points out something very interesting— that the command to respect one's mother and father[29] immediately follows the command to live a life of *kedushah*. This juxtaposition of verses comes to teach the sanctity and holiness of the act of creating life and of life itself. Because if life were to come from lust and not holiness, the child would have no reason to respect the parent. But when a child is born out of a holy impulse and the desire to emulate Hashem, the desire to give, love, and honor, then the respect of the child to the parent and the parent to the child is present. The Sefat Emet's interpretation of the Talmud's line "his interior matches his exterior"[30] is that a man's children are testimonies to his inner essence.

The *mitzvot* are our cheat codes to holiness. When we choose to be *shomer habrit* (careful of our covenant), we are choosing to live beyond our animalistic nature, to act in accordance with our infinite selves, our souls. All of nature can be used for darkness or for light. If we learned anything from Stan Lee and his Spider-Man comics, and I think we learned a lot, it is that "With great power comes great responsibility." We have the power, we have the potential, we even have the cheat codes. It's only if we use them and tap into the infinite part of ourselves that we become supernatural.

finding grace in time

Going through a break up can be one of the most difficult things to endure—it's a separation in what felt like a divine union; a heart shattered into a million pieces. But we have to find a way to trust that it is for our own good and what's truly aligned will arise at the right time. We have to shift our focus from what's lost and lean into faith that whatever is meant to be will be. We never know what our Creator has in store for us.

All of life in various ways, even if we don't fully feel it, is an element of heartbreak, since at all times we are somewhat separate from the *Shechinah* (indwelling, feminine Divine presence). How to elevate in exile is a part of the process of *Sefirot HaOmer*, rectifying each level of the seven *sefirot* of חסד, *chesed* (loving-kindness) through מלכות, *malchut* (sovereignty, leadership).

The Process of a Pure Personality

We learn that "the Jews in Egypt were on the 49th level of impurity," a step away from the bottom, the 50th level of impurity (tied to our animalistic soul and selves).[1] As everything has a balance and every potential for bad has the potential for good, we also learn that in these 49 days, *B'nei Yisrael* reached the very highest level: "the Jews were on the 49th level of holiness (tied to our Godly selves and souls) when they received the Torah," one step away from the highest level, the 50th gate/level of holiness, which was the revelation at Sinai.[2]

We are now in the midst of counting the 49 days of *Sefirat Omer*, from the second night of Pesach until Shavuot. The Omer is also referred to as Seven Shabbatot. And, as Rebbe Nachman says, we do it *"Peh Sach,"* meaning with an "open mouth." We are speaking spirituality into existence, mirroring the journey of *B'nei Yisrael* in the desert, who spent these 49 days in spiritual preparation.

With each day and week in these seven weeks, we are tasked with transcending our physical constraints and reaching redemption. Time is a figment of a fractured world, but it is the world we live in, and to remove the layers of *klipah* (the "shells" of everything around us that conceal Godly light), we need to go through the process of these seven weeks of counting, of meditation, of moving through seven Shabbatot until reaching the 50th day, when we receive the Torah anew.

Sefirat HaOmer is a journey in refining the seven emotional attributes outlined in the ten sefirot: חסד, *chesed* (loving-kindness); גבורה, *gevurah* (justice, strength, discipline); תפארת, *tiferet* (beauty, harmony, compassion); נצח, *netzach* (endurance, victory); הוד, *hod* (humility, empathy); יסוד, *yesod*, (bonding, foundation); and מלכות, *malchut*, (sovereignty, leadership).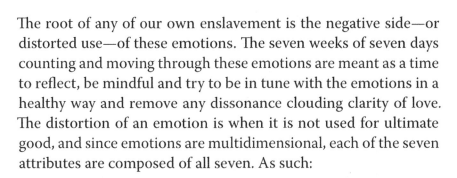

The root of any of our own enslavement is the negative side—or distorted use—of these emotions. The seven weeks of seven days counting and moving through these emotions are meant as a time to reflect, be mindful and try to be in tune with the emotions in a healthy way and remove any dissonance clouding clarity of love. The distortion of an emotion is when it is not used for ultimate good, and since emotions are multidimensional, each of the seven attributes are composed of all seven. As such:

> *Day One: Chesed of Chesed*
> *Day Two: Gevurah of Chesed*
> *Day Three: Tiferet of Chesed*
> *Day Four: Netzach of Chesed*
> *Day Five: Hod of Chesed*
> *Day Six: Yesod of Chesed*
> *Day Seven: Malchut of Chesed*

And this continues on Day One of Week 2: *Chesed of Gevurah*, and so on. To fully refine any one emotion, which would in theory take seven days, instead we count seven cycles of seven days.

In this time, we try to transcend our limited view of our physical reality and tap into our spirit that's beyond these constraints. We say the *bracha* (blessing) and speak the cycle into existence with *kavanah* (heartfelt intention). The Talmud teaches: "A person's prayer is not heard on high unless he places his soul in his hands."[3] This is a time to tap into transcendence. The *klipot* that manifest all around us represent the external, mirroring the negativity or egocentricity that keeps us from connecting to the internal and our true selves as creations with a Divine purpose, which connects us to the Divine light. It is the concealment that allows free will. It is the truth that is hidden that we have to fight to remain in to continue to do good and feel oneness. This negativity or ego is like the shell of a fruit: it does serve to protect the fruit, just as there are times it is useful for our own self-preservation, but it, too, must be removed to get to the sweetness. Focusing on the shell while ignoring its core will deceive us every time, leaving us holding the peel instead of its precious fruit. We have to remove our layers of ego and negativity to get to the root of our being and purpose, to get to a redemptive state and to receive the Torah.

Just last week, as I contemplated *klipah* as a concept and how it plays a part in our own lives, I wrote down a poem that went something like this:

> *this shell covering your magic*
> *if you can only see what I*
> *sea*
> *full of life that can't survive up here*

the inside of you under layers of fear

a fishbowl

a figment

one in your mind

peel

push

feel

rush inward

your outside is created

dig deeper to

being

a creation

sweet and pure as a fruit

but your shell has toughened

peel it all away

until you see

it was all a trick you played.[4]

Sefirat HaOmer is an opportunity for us to peel away the layers of the shell and move toward our inner essence, connecting to our Godly soul, instead of limiting our perceptions and actions to our Animal soul.

Moshe took *B'nei Israel* from *Mitzrayim* (מִצְרַיִם, Egypt), out of *meitzar* (מֵיצָר, a narrow constricted place), the definition of exile— spiritual narrowness and constrictions (*tzimtzumim*). He brought them to the border of the Promised Land. His purpose was fulfilled, and it's now our task to leave our own *Mitzrayim*, our own constrictions and enslavements, that which holds us back from reaching our potential and ascending to our personal Promised Lands. To bring on *Mashiach*, we have to make a redemption that is *prati* (private/personal) before we can see the final redemption that is *klali* (public/communal). It is on all of us, which is why in the pasuk commanding the counting, it is written, "yourselves." As is stressed in the Talmud, "each individual should count."[5]

> *You shall count seven full weeks for yourselves, from the day following the day of rest, from the day on which you bring the Omer as a wave-offering. Count fifty days, until the day following the seventh week.*[6]

'Shabbat' in Hebrew is etymologically related to the word *lishbot*, which means "to rest." Hashem commands us to rest in order to rise. If we hope to rise above nature and elevate our spirit, we have to rest from trying continuously to control the physical world. If we want to transcend and connect to our soul over our body, we have to pause our pursuits and connect to our purpose. *Sefira* is a count and practice of being mindful of the time around the seven opportunities (Shabbatot) to do exactly that, in hopes of doing our part from below, transcending the animalistic aspects of ourselves and connecting to the Divine within us, peeling away the layers of *klipah* so that Hashem answers from above on the 50th day with our key to redemption, the Torah.

A Festivus for the Rest of Us!

In these *parshiot*, the word Shabbat in relation to the festivals is recurring, but as we know, the festivals are less strict than Shabbat. No work may be done on Shabbat, but one is allowed to prepare food on the festivals. The ramifications of not observing Shabbat are far greater than those for not observing a festival. But, because the festivals are also referred to as 'Shabbat', the potential for spiritual connection and unification is beyond measure, because of the special space these days hold in time, their separation from elements of space and creation itself.

You have probably gotten a sense reading these *divrei Torah* how much I love Shabbat. Just feeling connected to Hashem, disconnecting from the everyday world, meditating on having been created—it's an incredible, ineffable feeling. In this *parashah* of Emor, Hashem gives us the commandment of Shabbat and of the Festivals, which are also referred to as Shabbat, "a holy occasion... a Sabbath to the Lord in all your dwelling places."[7] We are commanded to join in a Shabbat *to* Hashem. So, what's it all about?

We learn from the Holy One that words create worlds. In the beginning, Hashem *spoke* existence into being. *Tefillah*, prayer, is our daily method of emulating the Creator, speaking spirituality into reality. But on Shabbat and the festivals, we can focus on just that, without the constant distractions pulling us away from this unification. It's taught that on Shabbat we gain a *neshama yetera* (additional soul), and that this extra *neshama* allows a person to understand the mysteries of the Torah, so their *tefillot* (prayers) and learning are elevated.

The Restoration of Our Spiritual Selves

The Kabbalah teaches us about five worlds, which are a model for living a whole and balanced life, experiencing harmony between the body, mind, heart, and spirit:

> *Adam Kadmon (Primordial Man) – Will, Luminous Light*
> *Atzilut (Emanation) – Mind, Spirit, Soul*
> *Beriyah (Creation) – Thought, Intellect*
> *Yetzirah (Formation) – Heart, Feelings, Speech*
> *Asiyah (Action) – Body, Physicality*

The Hebrew word for universe is *olam*/עולם and is derived from the same root *alam*/עלם, which means to be concealed.[8] This is to hint that Hashem, who is King of the Universe, has hidden himself in the universe. These worlds above act as "garments" for Hashem's light.[9] As King David sings of creation in Tehillim, "You have dressed Yourself in majesty and splendor; You have covered Yourself with light like a garment.[10]"

Rabbi Aryeh Kaplan teaches: "The five universes are often explained in terms of their parallels at the human level. Man's innermost will and volition correspond to the universe of *Adam Kadmon*. The level of preconception or undifferentiated mind corresponds to *Atzilut*. The process of thought corresponds to the universe of *Beriyah*. Speech and communication parallel the universe of *Yetzirah* and, finally, action corresponds to *Asiyah*.[11]

Rabbi Shalom Sharabi points out that on Shabbat, the world of *Atzilut* (Emanation) shines into the world of *Beriyah* (Creation), meaning that the intellect is imbued with Divine consciousness that transcends intellect. So, when we study Torah on Shabbat, we can actually sense God's presence in it.[12]

I think Abraham Joshua Heschel articulates the power and feeling of Shabbat best many times in his book, *The Sabbath*, but one particular passage that jumps out to me is this:

> *All days of the week must be spiritually consistent with the Day of Days. All our life should be a pilgrimage to the seventh day; the thought and appreciation of what this day may bring to us should be ever present in our minds. For the Sabbath is the counterpoint of living; the melody sustained throughout all agitations and vicissitudes which menace our conscience; our awareness of God's presence in the world.[13]*

Rambam and Ibn Ezra point out that the word 'Shabbat' is used to describe a full week and not just Shabbat itself[14] In Vayikra, the Torah refers to Rosh Hashanah, Yom Kippur and Sukkot as Shabbaton and as Shabbat Shabbaton (a grand Shabbat)[15].

So we see that Shabbat and its power for connection and unification is constantly commanded to us. In this *parashah*, Hashem tells Moshe to speak to the Children of Israel and say to them, "Hashem's appointed Festivals, which you shall designate as callings of holiness—these are My appointed Festivals."[16] The entire Torah is *callings of holiness*, occasions to access what I like to call the "cheat codes to holiness".

We have previously learned about making time itself holy by partnering with God in observing Shabbat. This week, we learn how to designate time and space as holy outside of Shabbat as well:

שֵׁשֶׁת יָמִים תֵּעָשֶׂה מְלָאכָה וּבַיּוֹם הַשְּׁבִיעִי שַׁבַּת שַׁבָּתוֹן מִקְרָא־קֹדֶשׁ כָּל־מְלָאכָה לֹא תַעֲשׂוּ שַׁבָּת הִוא לַיהֹוָה בְּכֹל מוֹשְׁבֹתֵיכֶם

[For] six days, work may be performed, but on the seventh day, it is a complete rest day, a holy occasion; you shall not perform any work. It is a Sabbath to the Lord in all your dwelling places.[17]

אֵלֶּה מוֹעֲדֵי יְהֹוָה מִקְרָאֵי קֹדֶשׁ אֲשֶׁר־תִּקְרְאוּ אֹתָם בְּמוֹעֲדָם

These are the Lord's appointed [holy days], holy occasions, which you shall designate in their appointed time.[18]

These two sentences in Emor demonstrate the interrelationship between the finite and the infinite in such a perfect way. First, we are reminded that Shabbat's designation of time is *from* Hashem and remains consistent—a taste of the infinite given to us in our physical dwelling in time and space, on the 7th day of each week. The sages call Shabbat 1/60th of the World To Come. Then, we are introduced to the festivals (the High Holidays), which act like a Shabbat *for* Hashem, and *we* are tasked with designating the proper time for these holy encounters with Hashem.

This power that we are imbued with to sanctify time is made even clearer when we think about how those times are designated. The dates of the festivals are always correlated with the new moon (Rosh Chodesh). Rosh Chodesh is determined by the Rabbinical court in Jerusalem when two witnesses see a sliver of the moon, come before the court, and say, "*mekudash, mekudash*" ("sanctified, sanctified")[19] Then, as a community, we give thanks for the reappearance of the moon by reciting the *Kiddush Levana* (Sanctification of the Moon) blessings. So, these rituals that are grounded in our physical experience literally determine when Hashem's festivals will happen.

This restoration of our spiritual selves is also central to the rituals of the festivals. The High Holiday festivals fall on either the 30th or 31st day from the previous new moon. So, the exact timing is determined by us as part of the living Torah, unlike Shabbat, which has been set since the beginning and will be consistent until the days of *kulo Shabbat* (entirely Shabbat). Our sages refer to that time as the Messianic era, when darkness will fully be transformed to light.

Rashi points out that the commandment for festivals immediately follows a reminder and repetition of the holiness of resting. It's taught that whoever profanes the festivals by working on them is considered as though he profaned Shabbat, and whoever observes the festivals by "resting" on them is considered as though they observed Shabbat.

An Eternal Truth

It's interesting that in this *parashah*, as is the case in the rest of the Torah, the festival of Shavuot is not referred to as the time when we receive the Torah. We know that Shavuot correlates with the revelation at Sinai only from our oral tradition (*Torah Sheba'al Peh*). Akeidah gives two important perspectives on why this is the case. The first is seen in the fact that the existence of Hashem isn't mentioned in the 613 mitzvot, because had there been no Hashem to command them, there would be no reason to observe them. It's a given that they come from Hashem. The same applies to the giving and receiving of the Torah: the Torah is the first fundamental of Judaism, and the very fact that thousands of years later we observe it means it is a given that it was received. So, the Torah doesn't need to remind us. Furthermore, the receiving of the Torah doesn't depend on time, unlike other mitzvot. The Torah is, in fact, received at all times, as it's written, "This book of the Torah shall not depart from your mouth; and you shall meditate on it day and night."[20]

In the Torah and this *parashah*, Shavuot is called the holiday of first fruits and the wheat harvest. It is designated as a thanksgiving to the Creator who gives food to all. We see this in the following *pesukim* (verses):

> "And the feast of harvest, the first fruits of your labors, which you have sown in the field: and the feast of ingathering... when you have gathered in your labors out of the field";[21] "And you shall observe the feast of weeks, of the first-fruits of wheat harvest, and the feast of ingathering";[22] "Seven weeks shall you number unto you: Begin to number of the seven weeks from such time as you begin to put the sickle to the wheat."[23]

We *do* receive the Torah on this day in cyclical time, but The Abarbanel sees this as coincidental to the Festival, as the Torah itself is its own daily and perpetual remembrance. Rabbi David Zvi Hoffman says that it is not written that Shavuot is the time of receiving the Torah, because the vision of Sinai cannot be made into a concrete symbol.

The interplay between nature, creation, and spirituality is the constant dance of these *parashiot* and something in which we all struggle to find grace. The Abarbanel illustrates the mindful symbolism of these festivals: at Pesach, we are commanded to bring the Omer of barley, a grain normally used as animal fodder, which represents where we were as a people at Pesach—we hadn't yet received the Torah and were still trapped in the finite, animalistic ways of Egypt; on Shavuot, we are commanded to bring a *minchah chaddash* (new crop) symbolizing the new spirit that Hashem infused in us by giving us the Torah. And the counting of the Omer that we're doing between these two offerings is symbolic of our longing to achieve the clarity and connectedness with the Infinite, to not be stuck in nature and a place of finitude.

Shabbat and the festivals are moments in time to separate oneself from trying to conquer nature and tap into becoming supernatural. These are the moments that concealment is peeled back just a sliver affording us the opportunity to unify with Hashem, who is beyond space, time, and creation itself. Our character is weighed down by the harsh realities and *klipot* in this natural world. It is by virtue of these seven cycles of seven and the ritual of *Sefirat HaOmer* that we go through the process of refining our own character that brings us closer to the 50th gate of holiness. 50 being the number and notion that surpasses the natural world. The 49 days of our working through the constrictions of our Animal soul to connect to our Godly soul and the Infinite Light brings the redemptive Divine Light itself.

all reap, no sow

Let Go, Let God

All of life is about the beautiful balance of releasing control and connecting. Because we are tasked to "toil for our bread," we find ourselves stuck in a mindset of thinking that we are in control of our lives; that the more that we dominate our circumstances, the more in control we are. What we find in the lessons of *Shemittah* (the year of release, the sabbatical year) is that the rewards come from the release. Yes, we must work the field, so to speak, but without pause, there is no ultimate pleasure. To demonstrate faith to ourselves and our Creator, we have to pause our compulsion to constantly control. What we see most immediately with Shabbat, especially in the era of mini computers in our hands almost constantly, is that while we seem to be steering the ship, the ship often steers us. When we shift the dynamics and put away our machines, we can reconnect to our true purpose, our Creator and faith itself. It's like a hard reset to wash away the layers of disconnect, so that we can once again feel unified with our Source.

In the last *parashah*, we discussed Shabbat as a day of rest for Hashem and for us, and covered the *Shalosh Regalim* (the Three Pilgrimage Festivals), which the Torah also calls Shabbat, days of rest. In this *parashah*, *Behar*, we are taught about Shabbat for the land of Israel: for six years we may sow the field, prune the vineyards, and gather crops, but in the seventh year, the land shall have "a Sabbath of complete rest, a Sabbath for Hashem; you shall not sow your field or prune your vineyard.... A complete rest for the land." This seventh year is called the *Shemittah* year, the year when the land is "released."[1]

We also learn in this *parashah* that the Jewish people are commanded, when they go into the land of Israel, to count "seven sabbaths of years, seven years, seven times; and the days of seven sabbaths of years shall be for you forty-nine years."[2] The Torah goes further, instructing us to "sanctify the fiftieth year ... and proclaim freedom throughout the land for all its inhabitants."[3]

Reb Natan reminds us that after Adam ate from the Tree, the curse of toiling the land came into play. The mitzvah of *Shemittah* rectifies Adam's sin by ceasing to toil the land.[4] The most beautiful part of *Shemittah* is that every seven years we are commanded to forgive all debts, to not work the land of Israel by planting or harvesting, and to let all of the produce that grows become *hefker* ("ownerless"), so that anyone can take and eat from it. This rectifies the sin of Adam, who separated from Hashem by defying His word. By observing *Shemittah*, we show our connection to Hashem and the *mitzvot*, which acts as a *tikkun*. Beyond the unification with our Creator is a unification with each other, the notion of all that we have worked for in the land becoming ownerless shows that we all share equally in the benefits, demonstrating that the separations are human-made, and, in fact, we are all truly united.

It's a time when we transcend all economic and social differences. As we read, "The Sabbath produce of your land shall be yours to eat, for you, for your slave, and for your maidservant; and for your laborer and for your resident who dwell with you. And for your animal and for the beast that is in your land."[5] Just as Shabbat is 1/60th of the world to come, so, too, the year of *Shemittah*, when we stop working the field, gives us a taste of the world beyond our finite one. Where all beings, including animals, and rich and poor alike, have access to the complete harvest.[6] It is a time when the figments of our fractured perceptions and differences between each other fall by the wayside and when we share status, all being infused with Godliness of equal standing.

Taking this a step further with *yovel* (the Jubilee year), in the 50th year, the land of Israel again must lie fallow; it may not be worked. And all land in Israel that was purchased in those fifty years is returned to its original owners, in addition to the cancellation of all debts and the freeing of all slaves. These laws pertain to the land of Israel, as it says, "Take off your shoes from your feet, for the place upon which you are standing is holy ground."[7]

The Cyclical Nature of Seven

It is no coincidence that we read this *parashah* at the same time that we're counting the Omer—49 days (seven days for seven weeks) from Pesach to Shavuot, the 50th day, which kabbalistically represents the 50 Gates of Understanding (*binah*). The cycle of seven is seen throughout our lives: the two seven-day festivals—Pesach and Sukkot; marriage is celebrated and sanctified via the *sheva brachot* (seven blessings); *shiva*, the mourning period of a loved one, is seven days. Seven days is the count of clean days around *niddah* (women's menstruation), and, of course, the sanctification and inauguration of the Sanctuary (*shiv'at yemei milluim*), and the period of purification we undergo in the times of the Beit HaMikdash when we count from *tomeh* (impurity) to *tahor* (purity). And related to the time of *Sefirat HaOmer*, the splitting of the sea took place seven days after the Exodus. And the giving of the Torah happened seven weeks after Exodus. Seven is a cycle and a space where we can rectify the natural, and in that rectification, we are answered with revelations of Divinity.

As we covered in the last chapter, *Sefirat HaOmer* is a journey in refining the seven emotional attributes outlined in the ten sefirot חסד, *chesed* (loving-kindness); גבורה, *gevurah* (justice, strength, discipline); תפארת, *tiferet* (beauty, harmony, compassion); נצח, *netzach* (endurance, victory); הוד, *hod* (humility, empathy); יסוד, *yesod*, (bonding, foundation); and מלכות, *malchut*, (sovereignty, leadership). Seven is the DNA, so to speak, of creation, and the seven *sefirot* permeate the seven days of creation and are the ways in which Hashem orchestrates existence. We see this in ourselves, created in the Holy One's image, as we are composed of the seven attributes that we rectify during the Omer: love, restraint, harmony, ambition, devotion, connection and receptiveness. The Arizal explains that true "freedom" is the release of consciousness from its constricted state, the ability to approach Divine understanding of the world.[8] Both *Shemittah* and *Sefirah* are opportunities for us to rectify our base nature towards Divine understanding.

Rashi asks why the connection between *Shemittah* and *Har Sinai* (Mount Sinai), and as a response, the Chatam Sofer draws a parallel between the year of *Shemittah* and every day of the annual *Sefirat HaOmer* period. Each *Shemittah* consists of seven years and is followed by the 50th year, *yovel*. The seven weeks of seven days of *Sefirat HaOmer* prepare us for receiving the Torah when the shofar blasts, just as it does on Yom Kippur of the *yovel*. And as we read in Shemot: "Upon an extended blast of the shofar, they may ascend the mountain (בִּמְשֹׁךְ הַיֹּבֵל הֵמָּה יַעֲלוּ בָהָר)."[9] We see the connection between *yovel* and *Har Sinai*, as the shofar blasts at *Har Sinai* were described as *yovel*. In this *parashah*, we read that every seventh year was called *Shabbat Haaretz* (the Sabbath of the Land). This parallels every seven days of *Sefirat HaOmer*, which contains a Shabbat.[10] So, the ultimate redemption comes by way of both the 50th gate of understanding, through *Sefirat HaOmer* (Seven Shabbatot), of our inner selves leading to Shavuot, and the seven cycles of *Shemittah* of that which surrounds us and how we elevate nature, leading to the ultimate redemption—*yovel* at *Har Sinai*.

The sages say, "Whoever sanctifies himself from below is sanctified from above." And this recurring pattern in the Torah does just that—six days and years of working in the natural world, a seventh day and year of rest in holiness, and then the multiplication of those seven days or years by another seven. All leading up to the eighth day, the 50th day, and the 50th year, numbers that represent time beyond nature, the time that Hashem intervenes on another level, connection beyond our limitations in this world.

We have a Shabbat in time (seventh day), in space (the High Holidays), and in both space and time (the *Shemittah* and *yovel*), all intended to take all that we put into creation, all the work we do from below, and return it to us in a time of rest and unification with the Divine. The eighth day and 50th day/year go beyond even that and hint towards a time when we won't be constricted or held down by this world and its toil, instead we'll be completely unified to purpose, oneness, spirituality. This is referred to as the days of *kulo Shabbat* (entirely Shabbat). Our sages referred to it as the Messianic era, when darkness will be fully transformed to light, and we won't have to toil for our food. As King David sings, "Let there be an abundance of grain on earth."[11]

Human Nature and the Cycles that Surround

The Akeidat Yitzchak says that *Shemittah* and *yovel* are "Windows to open blind eyes, which are immersed in the sights of the (immediate) time." All land becomes ownerless, so a person doesn't become enslaved by their own labor and puts their faith back into Hashem as the ultimate provider. One is reminded in this dramatic way to be content with keeping enough produce to sustain themselves and to not allow the desire for wealth to overpower all else. It's an incredible way to be mindful of human nature and the cycles that surround it, while meditating on the part of us, our *neshamah* (soul), that surpasses nature.

I love what Judith Shulevitz shared on this topic in *New York Times Magazine*:

> *I [often] think of something two rabbis said. Rabbi Judah Loew of Prague, best known for his tales of the Golem, pointed out that the story of Creation was written in such a way that each day, each new creation, is seen as a step toward a completion that occurred on the Sabbath. What was Creation's climactic culmination? The act of stopping. Why should God have considered it so important to stop? Rabbi Elijah of Vilna put it this way: God stopped to show us that what we create becomes meaningful to us only once we stop creating it and start to think about why we did so. The implication is clear. We could let the world wind us up*

and set us to marching, like mechanical dolls that go and go until they fall over, because they don't have a mechanism that allows them to pause. But that would make us less than human. We have to remember to stop because we have to stop to remember.[12]

The land can keep giving, and we can keep taking, just as we can keep lending and allowing other people to take on debt, even if we see that a person might not be able to pay us back. When that is the case, debts build up across a whole community, the land becomes burdened, without any way to release the tension, fear, greed. R' Nina Beth Cardin says that "*Shemittah* is a rehearsal of a new way, a time to practice living in a world of "enoughness," where each of us is filled and flourishes with enough, where disproportionate inequities would not, and could not, exist. And when *Shemittah* is over, and we re-enter the other six years, we take a bit of what we learned with us and put it into practice in our everyday life."[13]

Shemittah is a Divine imperative, a concept introduced with the words בהר סיני (on Mount Sinai), so we are meant to rest assured that, even though we are pausing from sowing the field, Hashem will provide. As we read:

וְצִוִּיתִי אֶת־בִּרְכָתִי לָכֶם בַּשָּׁנָה הַשִּׁשִּׁית וְעָשָׂת אֶת־הַתְּבוּאָה לִשְׁלֹשׁ הַשָּׁנִים

My blessings for you in the sixth year and it will yield a crop sufficient for the three-year period.[14]

In this *pasuk* (verse), Hashem addresses the worry people might have that they won't have sufficient provisions for the year of the *Shemittah* and the years after it. Hashem says that He will bless the land and that, miraculously, there will be three years worth of provisions to reap in the sixth year, just before the *Shemittah* year. Just as there was a double portion of *manna* on *erev* Shabbat when the Jews were in the desert, so too there will be extra produce before the *Shemittah* in the Promised Land, so the people can fully celebrate this moment of holy rest. We need to realize this is Hashem blessing us, it's not a product of nature, but produced by Divine blessings, it is similar to the blessings of *parnasa* (livelihood), we can do our part (*hishtadlut*), but for the blessings to be received it is ultimately in the hands of Hashem.

Historically, the first *Shemittah* took place after the destruction of the second *Beit Hamikdash* (Holy Temple). To this day, farmers in Israel are required to keep *Shemittah*, and the most recent one was from September 7, 2021 to September 25, 2022. *Yovel*, on the other hand, is not currently observed because the entire Jewish nation needs to be living in Israel for it to be in effect. Once the tribes of Reuben, Gad, and half of Menashe were exiled, 130 years before the destruction of the first *Beit Hamikdash*, the *yovel* could no longer be observed.

Nevertheless, the lessons of *Shemittah* and *yovel* are timeless. *Chinuch* teaches that *Shemittah* is meant to commemorate the renewal of the world by Hashem alone, to teach us to have *emunah* and *bitachon* (faith and trust) in God, on the one hand, and generosity, on the other. We fulfill these mitzvot by releasing our impulse to work the land excessively and control creation. We release ownership and debts to ones in need, shifting our focus and trust in our own work and control and putting faith in the Divine will. It is a profound illustration of our faith that, after all, everything belongs to the Master of it All, Hashem.

Release control and connect.

faith fuels the future,
fear stirs the past

When Jon Batiste won the well-deserved Grammy for Best Album, his speech was beautiful. He got up there, and in such an *aidel* way, shared: "Wow. Wow. Thank you. You know I really, I believe this to my core: there is no best musician, best artist, best dancer, best actor. The creative arts are subjective and they reach people at a point in their lives when they need it most. It's like a song or an album is made, and it almost has a radar to find the person when they need it the most. I mean, man. I like to thank God. I just put my head down and I work on the craft every day. I love music. I've been playing since I was a little boy. It's more than entertainment for me; it's a spiritual practice. And there's so many people that went into making this album. My grandfather's on the album, my nephews, my dad is here. My executive producer, Ryan Lynn, right here. Come here, man. I don't want to just be up here by myself. I didn't do it by myself."[1] Then Ryan Lynn, who lives in my neighborhood, comes up wearing a *kippah*, hugs Jon and sits right back down.

It was a beautiful moment, a *kiddush* Hashem. What Jon shared is true: music, experiences and lessons do reach people in their lives when they need them most. That is the very definition of *Hashgacha Prati*/Divine Providence. A few days ago it hit me—faith fuels the future, fear stirs the past. When we experience something or resonate with something that speaks to an experience we are going through, it's human emotion and connection that validates some of our own hurt and healing. With that validation, we can realize everyone goes through it. And as Nas reminds us, "You gotta appreciate the moments; bad times don't last."[2] But we have to lean into faith that the heavy moments pass and open us up to a newer and better path.

The Benefits of Bitachon

Faith in the future brings the future we want. If we resist, we are blocking possibilities, but when we open ourselves up to the infinite architect behind the finite landscape, and don't let the past dictate our perception of the present, then we can actually manifest better for ourselves. It's when we stir in the past that fear blocks the infinite goodness that the future holds. When, in this *parashah*, Hashem mentions keeping the Divine statutes as a way for the rain to fall for us, it's because the rain is already for us, but for it to rain down blessings, we need to be open to it falling.

In the last chapter we covered the importance of releasing control and connecting, this being the purpose of Shabbat and Shemittah. This week with *parashat* Bechukotai ("My statutes"), we learn how to truly connect and how this unification brings blessings. It's funny because thinking of Jon Batiste's synchronicity and listening to Kendrick Lamar's new album, which has been speaking to me on many levels, I can't help but think of the chorus of "Die Hard," imagining it being a response to the first few *pesukim* of this *parashah*, singing out to Hashem:

> *I hope I'm not too late to set my demons straight*
> *I know I made you wait, but how much can you take?*
> *I hope you see the God in me, I hope you can see...*[3]

This *parashah* spells out the blessings that await if we follow what Hashem has laid out for us so clearly, if we focus on the part of us that is the Godly soul, but it also spells out what can happen if we disconnect from our Godly soul and become slaves to our animal soul.

אִם־בְּחֻקֹּתַי תֵּלֵכוּ וְאֶת־מִצְוֹתַי תִּשְׁמְרוּ וַעֲשִׂיתֶם אֹתָם....וְנָתַתִּי גִשְׁמֵיכֶם בְּעִתָּם

> *If you follow My statutes, and faithfully observe My commandments...I will provide you with rains in their season...*[4]

This is a curious verse, since if the purpose of it is to teach us to keep the *mitzvot*, then wouldn't it suffice to say "Follow my statues"?

It would seem superfluous to add "Keeping Hashem's commandments." This is a question by Sifri as stated by Rashi. The answer is that there is keeping the *mitzvot* and the action of doing or not doing what is commanded as *mitzvot ase* (the commandments to actively do) and *mitzvot lo ta῾ase* (the commandments to *not* do). The verse is meant to cover both the studying of the Torah and its *mitzvot* as well as keeping them *lishmah* (for their own sake) and for the sake of giving delight to Hashem.

Mitzvot are divided into three categories: *chukim, mishpatim,* and *eidot.* In the *pasuk,* it's written Bechukotai, which is the name of this *parashah,* and has the root of *chukim. Chukim* are the *mitzvot* for which no reason is given and we cannot rationalize. These are a distinct minority in the Torah. The overwhelming majority are of the other two categories, as the Torah was given in a way for human beings to comprehend. The most enigmatic of these *chukim* is the ritual of the *Parah Adumah,* the red heifer, which was used for ritual purification.

Mishpatim are rational *mitzvot* and, even without the Torah, would eventually surface as the only sustainable societal precept. This includes the commandments against theft and murder. *Eidot* are the *mitzvot* that are dedicated to remembering events and/or ideals. This includes observing Shabbat as a reminder of God creating the world, just as Pesach is a reminder of the Exodus from Egypt. These are not practices we would have necessarily thought of ourselves, but they are logical, unlike *chukim* that are beyond our comprehension.

Interestingly, it happens to be in *parashat* Mishpatim that I wrote, "It seems that we are all in various states of Divine disconnect. Some might even say we are spiritually sick. We attempt to heal, but it is a long journey and often feels impossible. When we attempt to heal our physical selves, it is in much the same way of doing and then hearing/seeing/understanding—when a doctor prescribes the medication we need to heal ourselves, we take it in good faith; we don't first go to medical school, researching every element of it and only take the medication afterward. If that were the case, we would remain sick, no doubt getting worse and worse. We take it in faith, because it benefits our physical selves and isn't contingent on our knowledge of its inner workings. In fact, by taking it, we can start to see clearer, feel better, and get a better understanding of how the medicine helped.[5] It is the same with our spiritual selves—the more we are in the space of *na'aseh v'nishma (we will do and we will listen/learn)* with the *mitzvot*, the more elevated our spirit, and by virtue of that, our physical selves, will be."

That is the emphasis on *Bechukotai* and *chukim*, as even the *mitzvot* that we cannot rationalize or comprehend, even those we most follow, for in those we can show our full faith, connect and reap the benefits both in this world and the next.

In Lukkutei Torah, the Alter Rebbe interprets the term *bechukotai* as related to the word *chakikah* which means "engraved." This is meant to teach us that not only are we commanded to keep the mitzvot, but we have to labor in the study and learning of Torah until it is engraved within us. We write the letters of the Torah on parchment, and though independent of the parchment, they become united with it. That is the process of continuing the tradition of writing the Torah. Engraving on a deeper level is when the letters are not an independent entity, as they cannot be separated from the object they have been engraved into. The two become one and that is what *bechukotai* is about: it is when we become one with the Torah that is Hashem in this world.

Last week, I was going back to the beginning of Tanya where it teaches exactly this point in Chapter Four, Section Two, "Merging with God." Chapter Four discusses the importance of the "outer self," the "garments" of ourselves that we express through thought, speech and action. And it stresses the importance of it as completing the "inner self," which is intellectual and emotional conviction. To simply love and revere Hashem is not enough—Bechukotai comes to teach us the importance of expression, not only word and action, but through *dveykut* (a clinging which comes from a true understanding).

The Zohar teaches that "the Torah and God are totally one."[6] The Alter Rebbe expounds on this, stating that the Torah, which seems to be a glimmer of the Divine, is actually the wisdom and will of God, and so it is completely one with God. It seems counterintuitive for an Infinite Light to be one with a finite element on earth given for us, but that is what infinite transcendence is, as the Rambam says, "He and His wisdom are one." Hashem is simultaneously the knower, the power to know, and the known.

When Kendrick Lamar's song pleads, "I hope you see the God in me," it's alluding to the fact that we are all made in God's image and if we could remember that when we engrave ourselves with Torah, as the *parashah* insists, we become unified with our Source. We can become light and see the light in each other, and that brings blessings to us all. But this is only done when we tap into and focus on the part of us that is Godly and not the garment of it which is animalistic.

Rebbe Nachman reminds us that the purpose of this life is to uplift the physical and animalistic part of ourselves to serve our spiritual selves, and in the first *pasuk* of our *parashah*, immediately following the reminder to keep Hashem's commandments, we are told that blessings will follow. One can ask: Why the material blessings for spiritual pursuits? Why bless the body for the achievements of the soul, if the soul is more important and even a separate entity? The answer lies in the realities of this world, and that the soul cannot attain the spiritual heights by itself. In this world, it needs the body—the body is the garment that facilitates its elevation. It is indeed the only way for a person to remain in the physical world while engaging in spiritual devotion. It's the delicate balance of *ratzo ve'shov*, which means "to run and to return," which we covered in Acharei Mot. The physical act of eating keeps the body and soul together so that spiritual growth can take place. Rabbeinu teaches that if a person strives to find Hashem and is worthy, the person's eating can elevate them to a level of desire and will for Hashem that transcends many other spiritual attainments. In such a case, the person's physical desires not only support their spiritual longings but actually mirror them.[7]

The Reflection of Water

וְאִם־לֹא תִשְׁמְעוּ לִי וְלֹא תַעֲשׂוּ אֵת כָּל־הַמִּצְוֹת הָאֵלֶּה: וְאִם־בְּחֻקֹּתַי תִּמְאָסוּ וְאִם אֶת־מִשְׁפָּטַי תִּגְעַל נַפְשְׁכֶם לְבִלְתִּי עֲשׂוֹת אֶת־כָּל־מִצְוֹתַי לְהַפְרְכֶם אֶת־בְּרִיתִי: אַף־אֲנִי אֶעֱשֶׂה־זֹּאת לָכֶם וְהִפְקַדְתִּי עֲלֵיכֶם בֶּהָלָה אֶת־הַשַּׁחֶפֶת

But if you do not listen to Me and do not perform all these commandments. And if you despise My statutes and your souls detest My laws, so that you stop performing My commandments, you will have broken my covenant, I in turn will do this to you: I will wreak misery upon you...."[8]

It says in Mishlei, "As water reflects face to face, so does the heart of man to man."[9] There is a reciprocal relationship, the one bringing about the other. We mirror each other, just as one good deed brings another in its wake, the reverse is also true. As we read these *pesukim*, outlining exactly how to act in this world, and when that is aligned the blessings rain down from above, as water reflects water, the *pesukim* outline that if we deny the truth, the light, and life itself, in that sense, the same reflects back to us in this world.

There was a son of a *tzaddik*, ten years old, he loved to hear his father read the Torah, even when it was the *tochacha* (the vivid curses). One year, his father was sick and unable to read the *tochacha*, so someone else read the Torah in his place. When his son heard the *tochacha*, he fell to the ground and fainted. He was bedridden for months. Once recovered, he was asked why for the first time the *tochacha* had such an effect on him. He replied, "Every year, my father reads the *tochacha*, and when my father reads it, I hear only blessings."

We have to realize it is the same with us: when we recognize the "bad" is for our good, it is our Creator putting us through a lesson for our ultimate growth and to steer us back onto the right path. Then we are able to have the *emunah*/faith and *bitachon*/trust that it is all for our own good. Like a *tzaddik*, we can take any temporal misery with joy as the concealment of good that will reveal itself soon enough.

The Alter Rebbe explains that all the *tochacha* in this *parashah* are in fact blessings.[10]

The Tzemach Tzedek draws an analogy of this, as recorded in the Talmud, when Rabbi Shimon Bar Yochai sent his son to receive blessings from Rabbi Yonatan ben Asmai and Rabbi Yehudah ben Gerim. When his son returned, he complained that he did not receive blessings at all, quite the opposite, it felt more like *tochacha*. His father, Rabbi Shimon, replied that all their words were truly blessings, and as the Tzemach Tzedek explains, because the blessings were so sublime, they were only able to be expressed in such a way. The Talmud asks if they were so sublime that they needed to be disguised as *tochacha*, how could Rabbi Shimon interpret them so openly?

It's exactly this lesson that we learn in the Tanya: that afflictions and suffering in this world are really the goodness of the 'hidden world,' the aspect of the *yud* (י) and *heh* (ה) in the *Havayah* (the holy four letter name of Hashem, the Tetragrammaton), and it manifests as "a shade, and not as light and revealed goodness." The *Havayah* is broken into two aspects: the first, the *yud* (י) and the *heh* (ה), signify that which is concealed—levels or worlds so sublime that they are hidden and concealed in our current reality. The second half, the letters *vav* (ו) and *heh* (ה), represent the revealed levels or worlds that are able to manifest and be seen by us as good in our current reality.[11] When we accept the suffering in this world with *emunah* and even joy, then as it says in Shoftim, "They that love Him are as the sun going forth in its might,"[12] which is as the world to come, where the suffering we endure in this world will be seen for what it truly is: manifest goodness.

Rabbi Shimon bar Yochai's soul's mission was to reveal *pnimiut haTorah* (the hidden inner dimensions of the Torah), and in this, souls experience elements of the illumination reserved for the world to come in their present personification. For this reason, Rebbe Shimon was able to see the reality of the concealed blessings the Rabbi's had given to his son. We, of course, are not on the level of Rebbe Shimon and able to bring down the concealed in such a way as he did with the Zohar, but the lesson is that *tochacha*, which is seemingly only for our suffering, is actually for our ultimate good, and when we can truly believe that, then we can see the blessings that it will bring and exist in it with joy.[13]

The Root of Love

The two aspects of the *heh* (ה) in the Havayah bring to mind this necklace that I received this week. It's gorgeous and its meaning is deep, so I just had to have it after I saw my friend Joshua Reitzenstein wearing it. His story with this piece of jewelry (which you can see to the left) is pretty amazing.

Joshua was leading a Birthright trip and the kids saw him admiring the necklace, in a very deep and profound way, as if he was divinely drawn to it. They were able to feel the connection he had with it, and so they secretly bought it for him and gifted it to him on the last day of their trip. He wore it for years, and it always kept him connected to being of service and giving. After a few years, he lost the necklace. But then his grandfather came to him in a dream on Rosh Hashanah. Joshua explained to his grandfather how he had lost this precious necklace and just then his grandfather smiled and pulled the necklace out from under his shirt and put it around Joshua's neck and then, like Obi-Wan Kenobi, he suddenly disappeared.

His grandfather had passed away a few years earlier, and it was a gift to see him again. He woke up to the first rain of the season. The dream state was great, but he woke up with the necklace on his mind. Somehow, the designer, Avraham Loewenthal, heard this story and immediately sent him a new one.

Much like Bechukotai outlines the two ways we could choose to act in this world, one bringing blessings and the other blocking them, the necklace signifies how we can emulate our Source. The upper and lower *heh* (ה) depicted in this necklace and in the world are about giving, receiving, and oneness.

Kabbalistically, the letters that spell out the Divine name represent aspects of our inner consciousness: the upper *heh* (ה) represents our desire to give and the lower *heh* (ה) represents our desire to receive. Our Source perpetually gives without the need or desire to receive, and this correlates and is mirrored in the extent to which we give.

Meanwhile, the lower *heh* (ה) ascending to the upper *heh* (ה) represents our spiritual awakening to pure giving and unconditional love. This inner transformation when manifested enables us to experience the infinite goodness that is the source of all reality.

The lower *heh* (ה) is empty because if we focus simply only on receiving, we are hollow. When we recognize the giving nature of the universe and that it's imperative to be in alignment, we can discover that, as we attain deeper levels of giving and love, we attain wholeness and deeper levels of divine union. This is why the Hebrew word for love, *ahavah*, has *'hav'* meaning "to give" at its root.

It's only when we attach ourselves in such a way to our Source, through learning the Torah and keeping the *mitzvot lishmah,* that we can become love, become light and manifest blessings for ourselves and each other. Oftentimes, I'll free verse poetic around my *dvars* as I write. So, I thought to end this *dvar,* I would share this week's:

key

kabbalistic

concepts

I am all that I was and will be

a potential only in completion of She

AN INTRODUCTION TO KABBALAH ITSELF

The word **Kabbalah** means 'that which is received, or the root, *Kabal*, to receive.' The Oral Torah (*Torah sheba'al peh*) was traditionally transmitted by word-of-mouth from father to son and from teacher to disciple. The Torah has two parts: The "*Torah shebichtav*" (written law), which is composed of the 24 books of the Tanach, and the "*Torah sheba'al peh*" (oral law).

We read in Pirkei Avot as a principle of faith, Moshe "received" (*Kibel*) the Torah from Sinai and transmitted it to Yehoshua.[1]

Rabbi Yehuda HaNasi, over 1800 years ago, realized that because of all the hardships of Exile, the Oral Torah was in danger of being forgotten, and only if it would be put onto paper and passed down to the generations would it endure. He brought the top scholars of his generation together and compiled the Mishnah, which is the collection of all the oral teachings that preceded him.

Unlike the Written and Oral Torah which all are required to learn, the mystical portion of the Torah which is referred to as "Kabbalah" was only shared with a select few righteous individuals in each generation, exclusive to the brilliant minds in Torah. It's important to note that Kabbalah does not exist independently from Torah; it cannot be understood or learned separately. Kabbalah is the composite of the profound level of understanding of the Torah, the *mitzvot* and the architecture of the higher and lower worlds, our Creator and creation itself. It teaches how we are all a piece of God, and how that piece relates to reality beyond comprehension. In essence, Kabbalah is Jewish Mysticism, and like other mystical traditions, it rests on the truth that we (and all of creation) are all one with the Infinite One.

The majority of Kabbalah that has found its way into some of Judaism's mainstream teaching and writing is based on The Zohar

(Hebrew: זֹהַר, Zōhar, lit. "Splendor" or "Radiance") which is a commentary of the Torah. The Zohar, written in Aramaic, contains the illuminated insights of Rabbi Shimon bar Yochai, who is quoted throughout Mishnah and Gemara.

For most, the next name that comes to mind in relation to the Kabbalah is Rabbi Yitzhak Luria, the great Sage from the 16th century, who lived in Egypt and Tzfat, Israel. Known also as the Arizal, the "lion of blessed memory," or simply, The Ari. Lurianic Kabbalah is a system The Arizal developed out of the teachings from the Zohar. The Arizal believed that only a scholar deeply versed in the "revealed Torah" could possibly understand the "hidden Torah."

As time went on, more and more Kabbalistic concepts have filtered down into mainstream Judaism and have infused deep spiritual connection and understanding of the *simcha* (joy) embodied in the *mitzvot*.

The Arizal teaches that creation came about because Hashem has a fundamental desire to give.[2] Therefore, the natural state of being is one in which *chesed*, the bounteous and unlimited influx of Hashem's life and kindness, flows freely into the world, unhampered by either sin or *dinim* (judgment). One of the major ways to sweeten judgment (*hamtakat hadinim*) is *tzedakah*, as it transforms *dinim* into *chesed*. We are tasked to emulate these qualities.

In Mishlei (Proverbs) it says, "There is one who gives generously yet ends with more."[3] Focusing on what you don't have over what you do often blocks the blessings you can get. Focusing on what you can give; you turn yourself into a vessel for receiving.

Kabbalah teaches that the world was created first through ***Shevirat Hakelim***, the shattering of the vessels. The initial (finite) vessels of creation couldn't hold the (infinite) Divine light—and they broke, scattering shards in every corner of the world. So in every dark place and thing in the world is a shard of light waiting to be redeemed. Reb Natan taught that our highest task is to *choose* to see God's Light; to choose to let in and partner with Hashem, even when the Holy One is hidden. Our laws and customs, in ways so mysterious and in ways very obvious—literally turning our physical bodies into ritual spiritual objects—are the most powerful reminders we have to keep making that choice to strive for something higher.

This brings us to *The Sefirot*—the inner structure and make up of the universes (*Olamot*). Kabbalistically, there are five worlds, each one concealing more and more of the Infinite Light (*Or Ein Sof*), where our world has God's light nearly fully concealed. The Sefirot act as garments, just as a garment can both conceal and reveal, the Sefirot have the dual function of contracting and emanating light into our world.

The process of concealment or contraction (*Tzimtzum*) allows for our very existence in what would otherwise be all Light, this process of Divine self-contraction and self-limitation is what makes our worldly existence possible.

This series of intermediary stages is called **Seder Hishtalshelut** and it is through these stages where the Light contracts that makes the creation of the finite world possible. We refer to Hashem as Melech HaOlem, the King of the World. The Hebrew word for world is *Olam*, which etymologically is related to the word *helem*, meaning 'concealment'. The reality of it is, that Hashem, the Light of Infinite, is the King who hides in this world. Without the concealment of the Infinite Light, there would be no space for anything besides the Infinite Light and the level of concealment is such that it allows for our free will.

These ten *Sefirot* are the modes and attributes through which

Hashem manifests and through which we ascribe qualities to our Creator. Rabbi Chaim Vital teaches that, "The soul's light arises and flows from the light of the *ten sefirot* (Divine powers) themselves without any intermediary.[4]

The word *Sefirah* is related to the verb *lesaper*, which means to "express," implying that the function of a Sefirah is to express a certain attribute. It is also related to the word *sapir* (sapphire). A sapphire is a gemstone that is illuminating, and the Sefirot are the channel in which we receive from the Infinite Light. So the *Sefirot* both conceal and reveal the expressions of Infinite Light into our *Olam*.

The names of the ten *Sefirot* are:

(כתר) **Keter** Crown

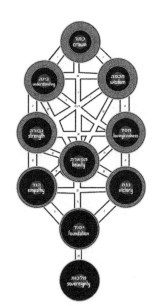

The Three Higher Sefirot

- *Chochmah*—wisdom (חכמה)
- *Binah*—understanding (בינה)
- *Daat*—knowledge (דעת)

The Three Lower Sefirot

- *Chessed*—loving-kindness (חסד)
- *Gevurah*—strength (גבורה)
- *Tiferet*—beauty (תפארת)
- *Netzach*—victory (נצח)
- *Hod*—empathy (הוד)
- *Yesod*—foundation (יסוד)
- and *Malchut*—sovereignty (מלכות)

In Kabbalah we see that the perfection of the first triad of the seven lower sefirot: *chessed, gevurah,* and *tiferet*, parallel the upper body.

The second triad, paralleling the lower body, is *netzach* (dominance), *hod* (empathy), and *yesod* (foundation). *Chesed* and *gevurah* are both related to giving. *Chesed* is giving freely while gevurah holds back from giving, as it is the practice of restraint and judgment. And the balance equals *tiferet*. We pray for the blessing of rain, but we need it given with restraint; too much rain would drown us all.

In Kabbalah, *yesod* parallels the sexual organ. This is the organ with which a person can both give and receive pleasure. *Yesod* represents a reciprocal relationship. Of course this, when perfected between a man and a woman, is the perfected state, one in which birth and creation manifest through partnership with the Creator. The one-way relationship exemplified by the first triad (*chessed*, *gevurah*, and *tiferet*) has to be perfected within oneself before hoping to perfect the reciprocal relationship exemplified by the second triad (*netzach*, *hod* and *yesod*). Rabbi Aryeh Kaplan illustrates the interplay of *netzach* and *hod* with a woman nursing her child: nursing is giving, but can nourish the mother as much as the baby.

The Process of a Pure Personality

All of life in various ways, even if we don't fully feel it, is an element of heartbreak, since at all times we are somewhat separate from the **Shechinah** (Divine Presence). How to elevate in exile is a part of the process of the *mitzvot* and in particular the focus of **Sefirot HaOmer** (counting the forty nine days from the second night of Pesach until Shavuot), rectifying each level of the seven *sefirot* of חסד, *Chesed* (loving-kindness) through מלכות, *Malchut* (sovereignty, leadership).

We learn that "the Jews in Egypt were on the 49th level of impurity," a step away from the bottom, the 50th level of impurity (tied to our animalistic soul and selves).[5] As everything has a balance and every potential for bad has the potential for good, we also learn that in these 49 days, *B'nei Yisrael* reached the very highest level: "the Jews were on the 49th level of holiness (tied to our Godly selves and souls) when they received the Torah," one step away from the highest level, the 50th gate/level of holiness, which was the revelation at Sinai.[6]

The Omer is also referred to as Seven Shabbatot. And, as Rebbe Nachman says, we do it "*Peh Sach*," meaning with an "open mouth." We are speaking spirituality into existence, mirroring the journey of *B'nei Yisrael* in the desert, who spent these 49 days in spiritual preparation.

With each day and week in these seven weeks, we are tasked with transcending our physical constraints and reaching redemption. Time is a figment of a fractured world, but it is the world we live in. We need to go through the process of these seven weeks of counting, of meditation, of moving through seven Shabbatot until reaching the 50th day, when we receive the Torah anew.

Sefirat HaOmer is a journey in refining the seven emotional attributes outlined in the ten sefirot: חסד, *Chesed* (Loving-kindness); גבורה, *Gevurah* (Justice, Strength, Discipline); תפארת, *Tiferet* (Beauty, Harmony, Compassion); נצח, *Netzach* (Endurance, Victory); הוד, *Hod* (Humility, Empathy); יסוד, *Yesod,* (Bonding, Foundation); and מלכות, *Malchut,* (Sovereignty, Leadership).

The root of any of our own enslavement is the negative side— or distorted use— of these emotions. The seven weeks of seven days counting and moving through these emotions are meant as a time to reflect, be mindful and try to be in tune with the emotions in a healthy way and remove any dissonance clouding clarity of love. The distortion of an emotion is when it is not used for ultimate good, and since emotions are multidimensional, each of the seven attributes are composed of all seven. As such:

Day One: Chesed of Chesed
Day Two: Gevurah of Chesed
Day Three: Tiferet of Chesed
Day Four: Netzach of Chesed
Day Five: Hod of Chesed
Day Six: Yesod of Chesed
Day Seven: Malchut of Chesed

And this continues on Day One of Week 2: Chesed of Gevurah, and so on. To fully refine any one emotion, which would in theory take seven days, instead we count seven cycles of seven days.

In this time, we try to transcend our limited view of our physical reality and tap into our spirit that's beyond these constraints. We say the *bracha* (blessing) and speak the cycle into existence with *kavanah* (heartfelt intention). The Talmud teaches: "A person's prayer is not heard on high unless he places his soul in his hands."[7]

This is a time to tap into transcendence. It is the concealment that allows free will. It is the truth that is hidden that we have to fight to remain in to continue to do good and feel oneness. This negativity or ego is like the shell of a fruit: it does serve to protect the fruit, just as there are times it is useful for our own self-preservation, but it, too, must be removed to get to the sweetness. Focusing on the shell while ignoring its core will deceive us every time, leaving us holding the peel instead of its precious fruit. We have to remove our layers of ego and negativity to get to the root of our being and purpose; to get to a redemptive state and to become the vessel which can receive the Torah.

Key Concepts Of The Two Souls

Rabbi Chaim Vital wrote in *Sha'ar Hakedushah* that every Jew possesses two souls, as it says in Isaiah, "And the *neshamot* (souls) which I have made."[8] The Alter Rebbe (Ba'al HaTanya) refers to these as the **Nefesh HaElokit** (our Godly soul which desires self-nullification towards a complete union with Hashem), our impulses to holiness and inclination to good. The Tanya begins by describing our Nefesh HaElokit as "a piece of God above"[9] and adds the word "literally," followed by the **Nefesh Habehemit** (our animal soul, which desires only its own self-gratification) and is steeped in egocentric impulses and negative inclinations. The *Tanya* teaches that one soul originates from the *Kelipah* (shell or peel): just as the peel conceals the fruit, Hashem conceals the Godly life-force within the shell of everything in creation. The other soul originates from the *sitra achra*, the side of creation that opposes holiness.[10]

The **Yetzer Tov,** the human inclination to do good, is rooted in our spiritual nature through our *Nefesh HaElokit* (Godly soul). Our bodies and the *sitra achra* ('side of impurity') find pleasure in conquering elements of this world, but our *yetzer tov* reaches beyond this world of concealment and wants only to unify with the truth—to elevate the concealing darkness by revealing the light within it. As King David sings, "My soul thirsts for You."[11]

The concept of *Nefesh HaBehemit* brings us to the **Yetzer Hara, Sitra Achra and Klipah**—Klipot are the opposing forces manifest as the *yetzer hara* (evil inclination). In the world, it's the outer coverings or "shells" that conceal Godly light. In ourselves, it is the negativity or egocentricity that keeps us from connecting to our true selves as creations with a Divine purpose, which connects us to the Divine light. This negativity or ego is like the shell of a fruit; it does serve to protect the fruit, just as there are times it is useful for our own self-preservation, but it, too, must be removed to get to the sweetness. In order to release the holy spark, the shell must be removed. We too have to remove our layers of ego and negativity to get to the root of our being and purpose.

The Zohar teaches that there are four kelipot, three of which are entirely evil and one of which is a shell that envelops the spark of holiness, this is called the **kelipat noga** and the Alter Rebbe discusses it in the Tanya. The *kelipat noga* is connected to holiness, but still balanced between good and bad, it is only the three that surround that are removed from holiness, which is the definition of *sitra achra*. The parts that pertain to the prohibitions of the Torah (i.e. forbidden objects, actions, thoughts, etc.) derive from the *sitra Achra*. While that which is permitted by the Torah (but is not specifically a commandment) derives from *kelipat noga*.

We see the power of the four elements— water, fire, earth, air— and how essential they are to each of us. Being surrounded by water and waves washing over us reminds us not only of the beginning, being in the womb and sustained by it, but being surrounded by the life-giving force that connects us all. It reminds us that we need to let go of all the little things we have created and strip ourselves down to the foundational elements and not all the traumas and experiences that create layers of shells around our true selves. These four elements in physicality have their counterpart in spirituality, the elements that compose the soul. It is these spiritual elements that bring life to the body and as everything has a balance, there is both positive and negative potential in these forces.

As King Solomon writes in Kohelet, everything was created one opposite the other (זֶה לְעֻמַּת־זֶה)[12] in perfect equilibrium in order for us to exist in free choice where in this world the positive and negative forces are balanced. This was the price for eating from the Tree of knowledge of good and evil.[13] Even in the ten *sefirot* of light and holiness there exists the opposite fueled by the force of the other side, the *sitra achra*.

The ten sefirot/powers within the *Nefesh Habehmit* are referred to in the Zohar as the ten crowns of purity,[14] While a crown is not attached to oneself, it influences one's thoughts. When we indulge in the crown of impurity, we are separating from our true essence and attaching ourselves to this outside influence powered by the *sitra achra,* which is anything which is not the holy side. Essentially, anything that is not serving our awakening, but so to speak, keeping us asleep.

Our task is to unify our disparate parts to serve Hashem with both our *yetzer tov* and *yetzer hara,* to make our animal soul, that desires to gratify physicality, subservient to our Godly soul that only desires to transcend the limitations of the finite and to unify with the infinite. With everything in creation we have a choice as to which soul we will approach it with. Our animal soul can use sex to try and satiate lust, or our Godly soul can use it to connect with a partner and, ultimately, emulate Hashem by creating life itself. We can eat food in a similar fashion to other creatures, or we can elevate the food by meditating on it, saying a blessing, realizing how incredible it is to be able to have what we need, using the strength the food gives us to continuously connect, learn and inspire others—all to bring light and truth into the *Olam*, pushing away concealment bit by bit. As King Solomon says, "don't strain the spirit with emptiness."[15]

It's wild to think that only about 3% of our brain processes are conscious (our thoughts, ideas, understanding, and our decisions), while the other 97% is used for subconscious and automatic functions. Our habits and beliefs also fall under the 97%, which kabbalistically is tied to our *Nefesh HaBehemit* (our animal soul), and illustrates the incredible power of the subconscious mind.

The 3% also corresponds to the three intellectual powers of *Chochmah, Binah,* and *Daat*—translated as wisdom, understanding and knowledge, which are an acronym for the word *ChaBaD.* The *ChaBaD* of the *Nefesh Hasichlit* (the intellectual soul) is the conscious intermediary soul, less subjective than the *Nefesh HaBe-hemit* and not as transcendent as the *Nefesh HaElokit* (Godly soul). In this way, the *Nefesh Hasichlit* is the bridge between the *Nefesh HaElokit* (which desires self-nullification towards a complete union with Hashem) and the *Nefesh HaBehemit* (which desires only its own self-gratification).

We need to use the intellect, the *Nefesh Hasichlit,* to color our subconscious towards good because even when our intentions in our conscious thoughts and ideas are for the best, our subconscious can sabotage them. The reason for this is because our subconscious doesn't actually work with reason or logic, but with images and emotions. So, if we understand in a given situation that there is nothing to be afraid of, but our subconscious mind pulls from past images stored in our subconscious mind, we will feel afraid nevertheless. Since the part of our brain in the back that our subconscious mind sits in takes up more than the part in the front that colors our consciousness, we need to be that much more careful to replace negative imagery with positivity. This is what will balance our conscious and subconscious and bring us closer to a space of tranquility, which brings blessings. *(Find additional info on the two souls below in the portion about the Shema.)*

The Divine Names

Hashem—When I use the word "Hashem" in many places throughout these pages, it is important to know that 'Hashem' literally means 'The Name' and is a euphemism for the Tetragrammaton (*Yud-Kay-Vav-Kay*), which is never spoken as it appears in the Torah. This name is *kulo chesed*, complete kindness. The permutations of God's name give us clues into understanding aspects of God that are generally concealed. As it's written in Tikunei Zohar, "No thought can grasp Him at all."[16] And it is the same with the names we attribute. None of the names of God, refer to the Creator in the infiniteness beyond the reality of our own comprehension, they are simply names used throughout the canon of Judaic texts that we relate to the Divine as we experience and try to comprehend God in creation and in our present state of exile. When referring to the Creator beyond any attributes as we understand them, we use the term *Ein Sof*, which means Without End.

Throughout the Torah, we see the various permutations of Hashem's name and the power that each contains within it. The one name that we do not speak out loud, also known as the HaVaYaH (Tetragrammaton), is *kulo chesed*, full kindness. Others include *Elokim, Adni*, and *Ehyeh. Elokim* signifies Hashem's attribute of judgment and severity, while the name *Adni* signifies the attribute of authority and dominion ('*adon*' means 'master' or 'ruler'/'*adonai*' means 'my master').

These two names signify two types of courts: *Elokim* is that of strict judgment and is associated with the sefirah of *Gevurah*, and *Adni* correlates with leniency associated with the sefirah of *Malchut*. The name *Ehyeh* (אֶהְיֶה) is the mediator between *HaVaYaH*, on the one hand, and *Elokim* and *Adni*, on the other. This is why Hashem commands Moshe to tell the children of Israel that he's been sent by *Ehyeh*, the God that balances strength and kindness, judgment and mercy.

Rebbe Nachman explains that the secret of personal redemption is to combine *chesed* and *gevurah* in order to attain *Da'at* (Ultimate Knowledge/Wisdom). Loving kindness or judgment by itself is incomplete. Balance—knowing when to use each trait—is key. Tempering one over the other and the ability to know when to use each characteristic is *Da'at*.

In the Talmud it says, "A person should always draw people closer by means of his right hand and push them aside with his left hand."

As King David says in Tehillim, "The world was built with *chesed*."[17] *Chazal*, our Sages, teach that "The light that was created on the first day shone from one end of creation to the other," and in Kabbalah we learn that the light of *chesed* is contained throughout all of creation, as it says, "In the beginning, an infinite, uncompounded light filled all of Creation."

The sefira of *gevurah* represents restrictive power, limiting and concealing the Infinite Light, so that all creation receives in accordance with its capacity. Therefore, a balance of *chesed* and *gevurah* is necessary for *bearable* good to exist in this world. This is manifested in the sefira of *tiferet*, which represents the harmonizing of giving and restraint, so that a bearable amount of beauty and revelation can be seen in an *Olam* (world) that is *Ne'elam* (Hidden). To illustrate this a bit, we pray for rain because water is essential to life, but rain must be given with restraint because too much would drown creation. All good must be given with restraint. The word *tiferet* is derived from the Hebrew word *pe'er*, meaning 'beauty.' The more good and unification with the Divine source one can attain, the more hidden beauty from this world of concealment becomes revealed.

Ze'er Anpin: (Aramaic., lit. "the small face"); the term used by the Kabbalah for the Divine attributes which parallel emotions (the seven lower sefirot).

Nukvah—(the female of *Z'eir Anpin*, Aramiac for the Hebrew word, *Nekavah*, 'feminine', referring to *Z'eir Anpin's* bride) of *Z'eir Anpin* and that vows occur in the supernal *Ima* (i.e. *binah*).

Kabbalistically, the sun and the moon are associated with *Z'eir Anpin* and *Nukva*, respectively, (the bride of *Ze'ir Anpin* and the Aramiac for the Hebrew word '*nekavah*', meaning feminine). The coupling of *Z'eir Anpin* and *Nukva* represents the unification of emotion and expression. The radiance of the *Z'eir Anpin* shines as emotion, which is reflected in its counterpart, *Nukva*, which manifests its expression. This is seen in both how the moon reflects the sun and how Yehoshua's face showed his spiritual level as a reflection of Moshe's light.

I always found the *Leshem Yichud* verse—"For the sake of the unification…"—very powerful. Sephardim and some Chassidim traditionally say some form of the *LeShem Yichud* prior to doing any *mitzvah*. Chabad say it before *Baruch Sha'amar*, and that is meant to apply throughout the day.

לשם יחוד קודשא בריך הוא ושכינתיה, בדחילו ורחימו ורחימו ודחילו,
ליחדא יוד ק"י בוא"ו ק"י ביחודא שלים (ה')

For the sake of the unification of the Holy One, blessed be He, and His Presence, in fear and in love, to unite the Name Yud-Kei (the masculine part of the Divine), with Vav-Kei (the feminine part of the Divine) in perfect unity, in the name of all Israel.

This verse is meant to declaim the unification of the *Zeir Anpin* and the *Nukvah*. As a result of our spiritual exile, we are far removed from the Edenic state and our Godly souls. And so the *Shechinah* is not in a state of proper union with *Z'eir Anpin*. Reciting this verse with pure intention is meant to help rectify the disunity and concealment. The verse's power is filled with the reality of the entire purpose of the Torah, which is "for the sake of the unity of the Holy One, Blessed Be He (Z.A.), and His *Shechina* (Nukva)—the bride of *Z'eir Anpin* and the Aramiac for the Hebrew word 'nekavah', meaning feminine.

Other Terms And Concepts

Tohu and Tikkun: As described briefly above, Kabbalah relates that in the beginning of creation there was a breaking of the vessels (*shevirat hakeilim*) referred to as Tohu (chaos) when the light departed, as a sort of "destruction for the purpose of building." This is written about in the verse first two sentences of the Torah, we read, "The earth was without form (*Tohu*) and empty (*Bohu*), with darkness on the face of the depths. But God's spirit moved on the water's surface."[18] *Tohu* is literally translated as chaos, but is also understood to mean a "void" or "without form" and *Bohu* is translated as emptiness, alluding to a vessel which is ready to receive. Rabbi Aryeh Kaplan teaches that when separated, *Bo Hu* means "is in it"[19] implying its ability to hold the light "in it." Whereas *Tohu* is the state that leads to the shattering of the vessels, *Bohu* is the *Tikkun*, rectification of that state that leads to the vessels.[20] The sparks of light and holiness that "fell" from this shattering of the vessels are concealed in this world, and it is our task to reveal and rectify this through elevating ourselves, each others and the elements of this earth through the *mitzvot*, and our *ahavah* (love [of God]) and *yirah* (fear [of God]).

Shechinah ("feminine aspect" of the Divine): (the indwelling, but exiled "feminine aspect" of the Divine Presence): *Tohu* which was the process of the shattering and falling of the vessels was the first moment of the Divine in concealment which saw the *Shechinah* in a state of exile. The root of *Shechinah* is *shachan* meaning "to dwell," implying that the *Shechinah* is "dwelling" in a certain place, but it is this concealment of the Infinite Light in creation which allows for free will by hiding the revealed light of God within our current reality. The paradox is that God both fills all of creation and is in concealment simultaneously. The aspect of the *Shechinah* and its "dwelling" hints to the spiritual states where the Divine presence is more imminently felt. The Talmud describes the prophetic experience as the *Shechinah* resting upon the individual.[21]

The 16th century Kabbalists of Tzfat, led by the Arizal, felt the longing for the Shechinah so profoundly that they created a kind of cosmic wedding ceremony for the masculine and feminine aspects of the Divine, the great coming together of the primordial yin and yang—called Kabbalat Shabbat. It was these Kabbalists that brought back the concept of praying to the Shechinah, calling her by name. (More on this below.)

Alma D'itkasya **and** *Alma D'itgalya* (Hidden Worlds [the world of concealment] and Revealed Worlds [the world of revelation]): *Alma* is Aramiac for the Hebrew word for world *Olam*. These concepts encompass the spiritual realms in which the Light of the Infinite is concealed and revealed. The spiritual "worlds" are divided into these two categories by the Zohar and it's these worlds that are the root of both the hidden and revealed aspects and attributes of the ten *sefirot* as pertaining to the human system. The Zohar divides the many spiritual "worlds" into two general categories: the hidden world, called *"Alma D'itkasya"*, and the revealed world." These worlds are the primordial root of the hidden and revealed aspects of the human system. Hashem, (The Name, YHVH) known as *HaVaYaH* (Tetragrammaton) is the name of God which denotes the level at which the past (*HaYah* הָיָה), the present (*HoVeh* הֶיֶה), and the future (*YiHiYeh* יִהְיֶה) are one.[22] This name also denotes the creative power that constantly sustains the universe.[23] When this *Havayah* name is split in two: yud-hei (יה) and vav-hei (וה). Kabbalistically the. *yud-hei* (יה) embodies the upper spiritual and hidden world, and *vav-hei* (וה) the lower and revealed world.

Atik Yomin: (Aramaic, kabbalistic term; lit. "ancient days") this is a concept that transcends the ten *sefirot*, it's an inner dimension of *Keter*, an elevated level of spirituality that exists in complete oneness with the Infinite Light. *Atik Yomin* is mentioned in Daniel, "I saw the Ancient of Days sitting on a throne, His garment was white as snow, and the hair of His head was like pure wool."[24]

Dveikut: (lit. "clinging") describes spiritual attachment, a cleaving, and a unification to the Divine which stems from the attribute of *Yesod* facilitating a person's receiving more delight in serving Hashem than any other (physical) delight in this world.

Orot and Keilim: (lit. "lights and vessels") *Keilim* are vessels ready to receive the Divine light (energy) or emanations, the relationship between the two is that the light has to be channeled into *keilim* for it to effect creation.

Yichudim: The soul's rectification is that of *yichudim*, traditional Kabbalistic techniques of contemplating the union of specific divine names of God, referred to below as "mystical meditations." The word *yichud* means union and also denotes specialness, as it is related to the word *meyuchad*, and oneness, as it shares a root with the word *echad*.

Yichudim the soul's rectification of any division coming into states of unifying supernal elements, which is done in the lower realm with mystical meditations of the union of specific Divine names, and mystical devotions (kavanot) when engaged in prayer and/or the performance of *mitzvot*.

We see this when breaking down the word, *mitzvah*, looking at the word *tzavta* and *metzvaheh*. *Tzavta* means "being joined together" and *metzaveh* means, "the one who commanded it." From this we learn that through Torah and *mitzvot* there is unification and *dveykut* (a clinging, or cleaving to Hashem). The entire purpose of this world is to join created with the Creator, and transform our physical and spiritual selves into total embodiments of Torah and *mitzvot*—which is life itself. *Yichudim* is the act which describes a perpetual state of *teshuvah*, a return to our Source. Just as re-turn implies a prior turning, we see that *teshuvah* requires turning back, turning inward, to Truth.

Dirah b'Tachtonim: The chassidic concept of *dirah b'tachtonim (a dwelling for the Infinite Light in the lower realms)* is an oft-repeated teaching by the Lubavitcher Rebbe. It's expounded by the verse, "They shall make for Me a dwelling, and I will dwell amidst them (*veshachanti betocham*)."[25] Grammatically, the text should have said *"veshachanti betocho"*—"I will dwell within it [the Mishkan]." According to the Shelah (Sha'ar Ha'otiot, *ot lamed*), this indicates that in addition to building the physical *Mishkan*, Hashem wants every Jew to make themselves into a holy place so that the Infinite One can dwell inside. We are each tasked with building a personal Temple from the inside out. The more we work on building and revealing that holiness within ourselves and each other, the more Hashem's presence is fully revealed in the world (and the closer we get to the third and final Temple and redemption). The *chassidic* masters explain that this, "is what man is all about; this is the purpose of man's creation, and of the creation of all the worlds, supernal and terrestrial: to make for God a dwelling in the lower realms."

So, this system and teaching of *dirah b'tachtonim* shines light on the role of the physical *mitzvot*: that it is these acts that some might view as mundane and less spiritual that bring us to the greatest spiritual heights. It is the seemingly "lower" acts of worship that bring about the greatest unification with the Infinite Light.

Itaruta Diletata and Itaruta Dile'eyla are terms in Aramiac that mean an "arousal from below" and an "arousal from above."

In *Likutey Halachot*, Reb Natan expounds on the notion of opening one's hand to give charity, which he calls an "arousal from below" and the first step in repentance. This isn't exclusive to *tzedakah*, but when we perform *mitzvot lishmah* (for the sake of Heaven) which elicits a reciprocal response from Hashem. *Tzedakah* is a good example of a mitzvah that creates an "arousal from above." King David sings in Shir HaShirim, אני לדודי ודודי לי—*"I am my Beloved's and my Beloved is mine."*[26] The mystical interpretation of *"I am my Beloved's"* is an *"arousal from below"*— the Jewish people draw closer to Hashem while ‏ודודי לי‎, *"My Beloved is mine,"* is an arousal or revelation from above. To merit the revelation, each person must first awaken our own love and fear—this is "arousal from below." It is our spiritual task manifested through our offerings and the meticulous way in which we build the Mishkan (and our inner temples). The idea also plays out in *hashgacha*, Divine Providence, and *hashgachah pratit*, God's direct personal supervision. This is when one see's Hashem's ongoing active participation in one's life, the "arousal from above." This is when a person sees, as Ramban explains, Hashem choosing to reveal Himself to humankind. What each person does with that is up to them, but when a person *chooses to receive* that revelation and offers it back up in generosity, then we fully understand what the Rambam and the Rebbe explained earlier in relation to a *"dwelling for God"*—humans serve Hashem and create a dwelling for His revelation within themselves.

The concept of doing something *Lishmah* (for its sake) is a key concept in both living in alignment with oneself and living in alignment with our Source. It's the inner spiritual work, when done with the physical performance of a mitzvah, that sanctifies our outer being. The Zohar stresses that *ahavah* (love) and *yirah* (awe) are the two main ingredients needed for Torah and *mitzvot* to affect their ultimate purpose.

THE SHEMA—‏שְׁמַע יִשְׂרָאֵל ה' אֱלֹקֵינוּ ה' אֶחָד‎

"This Torah shall not be removed from your mouth"[27]

Rabbi Yochanan said in the name of Rabbi Shimon Bar Yochai that even if a person would just recite the Shema in the morning and the evening, he fulfills this *mitzvah* of "not removing the Torah from one's mouth." The lesson is that if you fall short of your goal, you have to focus on the good that you have done, because each person is only expected to do as much as they can, given where they're starting from. If they do that, it's as if that person has fulfilled all of Torah.[28]

I remember learning the power of the Shema (שְׁמַע) as a little kid. It felt like I was in the world of *Harry Potter* and someone had clued me into the Patronus charm, so if I put myself into a deep enough spiritual space, I would be able to conjure up protective power. The Shema was a way to channel Hashem's oneness into this world; I could say it and manifest magic in my own life. It was a pathway from the natural world I was in as a kid to the supernatural world that my kid mind dreamt up.

Growing up as a Yemenite Jew, I learned to form my hand into a *shin* (שׁ), the first letter of the Shema, by placing my thumb and pinky together, leaving my index, middle and ring fingers upright. Once I had this formation, I would close my eyes and place my pinky on my left eye and my thumb on my right. As I got to the last word of the Shema, *echad* (אֶחָד/'one'), I would bring all the fingers together, forming one unit and a sort of *daled* (ד), the last letter of *'echad'.* Then I would kiss my fingers and raise them to the heavens. It is a powerful ritual, one of connection and transcendence.

The Shema (שְׁמַע) is the climactic praise, prayer, and mantra that centers us in the morning and evening prayer. It's been at the center of Judaism and the lives of Jews since Moshe said the words to the Children of Israel in the desert thousands of years ago. It took on new levels of meaning when formal *tefillah* replaced the sacrifices, after the second Beit HaMikdash (Holy Temple) was destroyed by the Romans in 70 C.E. It is the climax of the final *Neilah* prayer on Yom Kippur, and oftentimes it is the last sentence a person utters before death.

The Shema has been echoing through Jewish generations for millennia, its kabbalistic powers potent with the preservation of a nation that introduced monotheism to the world. This sentence spells out the Oneness behind and within all of creation.

שְׁמַע יִשְׂרָאֵל ה' אֱלֹקִינוּ ה' אֶחָד

וְאָהַבְתָּ אֵת ה' אֱלֹהֶיךָ בְּכָל־לְבָבְךָ וּבְכָל־נַפְשְׁךָ וּבְכָל־מְאֹדֶךָ

Hear, O Israel! The Lord is our God, the Lord is One.

You shall love the LORD your God with all your heart and with all your soul and with all your might.[29]

The Zohar[30] teaches that affirming (ה') Hashem/Adonai and Elokim (אֱלֹקִינוּ or אלקים), the center of the Shema, is the general principle of all of the written and oral Torah and the foundation of all the *mitzvot* (commandments). The **Mitteler Rebbe**, Dovber Schneuri, elaborates that all of the Torah and *mitzvot* are included in the unity of the Holy One, blessed be He, and His presence in the world, which are the two names, Hashem and His title, Elokim.

The word Hashem literally means "the Name" and is a placeholder for the HaVaYah as it was pronounced back when the Temple stood. The name itself is actually a combination of the three words *haya*, 'past', *hoveh*, 'present' and *yih'yeh*, 'future'. *Chazal* (our Sages) teach that this name describes God a power that transcends the boundaries of time.

From Hashem's perspective, past, present and future are experienced all at once because Hashem is, of course, beyond the limitations of time. The Shema is a meditation manifested from this concept, revealing the reality that Hashem is beyond the boundaries of nature, including time.

Each time we recite this verse in prayer, we say in an undertone, "בָּרוּךְ שֵׁם כְּבוֹד מַלְכוּתוֹ לְעוֹלָם וָעֶד", "Blessed be the name of the glory of His kingdom forever and ever."

These two verses (Shema and Baruch Shem) are called *Yichuda Ila'ah* (The Upper Unity) and *Yichuda Tata'ah* (The Lower Unity), and the Zohar teaches that these two aspects of Hashem's unity are paradoxically beyond the world while simultaneously filling the world.

The first words, 'Shema Yisrael' are the key concepts prior to going into the permutations of Hashem's name. Shema means "hear" or "understand," as it's introducing a reflection, a meditation. The word Yisrael is the second name given to Yakov. Chazal teach that the two names, Yakov and Yisrael, represent two different spiritual levels. The name Yakov, derived from the word "heel," describes a state of constriction imposed by the outside world. Yisrael is made up of the words "master" and "head" and represents the mindset of being masters over our environments, learning to not be led or controlled by them.

The Sefirot in Kabbalah teach us about the upper and lower worlds of existence, but they also represent a person's existence, from head to toe, each aspect of the Sefirot correlating a physical element to a spiritual one. The words 'Shema Yisrael' are meant as a reflection on rising to the level of Yisrael, from heel to head, kabbalistically from *malchut* to *keter*. Each time we say these words, we are reminding ourselves that we do not have to be a product or victim of our environment. We can rise above nature by connecting to the supernatural, the Light of the Infinite.

Rebbe Nachman teaches that the Shema and Baruch Shem contain a total of twelve words, paralleling the Twelve Tribes of Israel, who parallel the Malchut of Holiness. The 12 words contain 49 letters which parallel the 49 letters in the names of the Twelve Tribes. When you recite these verses with all your heart and soul, you include yourself in the Malchut of Holiness and push away the sitra achra, which attempts to distance each of us from holiness.[31]

The Shema is a moment to get lost in love, but on a level greater than *ahava* (love); on this level of *dveikut*, cleaving to Hashem, which we could describe as *ahavah* in action. Rebbe Nachman teaches that the mitzvah of loving Hashem is the root of all the positive commandments—when a person acts honestly out of that love, it causes Hashem's name to be beloved and brings out the desire to fulfill all of the *mitzvot*.

Rambam in *Hilchot Teshuvah* expounds on the mitzvah of loving Hashem:

> *The proper love is that one should love Hashem with the greatest love, the strongest, to the extent that his soul is bound up in the love of Hashem, and the person thinks of this constantly, as if he is sick with love, where his mind is not free of the love of a woman, and he thinks of her constantly, whether he sits or gets up, or when he is eating and drinking. More than this should be the love of Hashem in the hearts of those who love Him, who think of [their love] always, as He commanded us, "with all your heart and with all your soul."[32] As King Shlomo articulated; "for I am sick with love."[33]*

The Dubno Maggid, a disciple of The Baal Shem Tov, gives an analogy where a certain villager brought a garment back to the tailor who made it and screamed that it was the wrong size. The tailor looked at the villager and burst out laughing. The villager had put the new garment on top of his old, tattered suit. The same is true with love. Love can only fill the heart that has room for it. If a person's heart is filled up already with fears and anxieties, or to put it another way, if a person's heart is closed, then it cannot be filled with love. This is what *Chazal* said in Sifri, "Do you not know how to love?" It states, "These words shall be…. on your heart."[34] This means that you actually have to make a place in your heart for these words, clearing away the *tum'ah* (spiritual impurity) and the dross of the *sitra achra*. This action is the one to fill your soul and to bring you to the taste of Supernal love.

Closing one's eyes to the physical world and tapping into *dveikut*, clinging to the Oneness, is what's needed to connect to what is beyond our purview. To pursue a real connection with the Divine, it's essential that we pause from our constant battle against time and reflect on what is beyond time. The proclamation of the Shema and Hashem's Oneness is meant as a reminder that all is God, so all is good. Our task to put our *emunah* (faith) and *bitachon* (trust) in the truth of the Shema and Baruch Shem, to release the control that we think we have and sing out that all is in Hashem's control, except our Love of Him, which is left to each of us to recite with all your *"heart and with all your soul and with all your might."*

We deepen the lesson of "not straying after your heart and eyes" during the ritual of *Shema*, as we cover our eyes with our right hand when we recite the first verse. The Hebrew word for 'eye,' *ayin* (עַיִן), sounds like the letter *ayin* (ע), which has a numerical value of 70. A person's eyes can lead them to the roots of the Torah, which are associated with the 70 members of Yaakov's household,[35] or they can lead a person astray, toward material desires, like that of the archetypal 70 nations of the world. Kabbalah explains that there were 70 *Nefashot* (souls) who descended to Egypt, which counter the 70 ministers of the non-Jewish nations. The numerical value of the Kabbalistic concept of *Sod* (secret) is 70, which represents the lower seven *sefirot* (*i.e. chesed, gevura, tiferet, netzach, hod, yesod, and malchut*) included within the ten *sefirot*. So, when we close our eyes and meditate on speaking out this mantra of *Shema*, we are reaffirming our faith and transcending material desires towards a unification with Divine consciousness.[36]

In the verse above and in the *Shema*, you may have noticed when it says heart—לְבָבְכֶם (hearts), it's actually plural. Each person has two conflicting inclinations, which the "two hearts" in this verse allude to. As we covered above, we all have a *Yetzer Tov*, our Godly soul, that wants to connect to the Light of the Infinite, gratified only through Godliness and, on the other hand, we have the *Yetzer Hara*, our animal soul, the part that is tied to the physical, that is connected to the finite, that wants to immerse itself in all the pleasures of this world, gratified only through the self. (More on this in the previous section on *yetzer tov* and *yetzer hara*).

The Alter Rebbe teaches in Tanya that the *Shema* prayer in particular is an opportunity for focused meditation that can bring a *mochin de-gadlut* (expanded consciousness) of the Supernal mind. It's a time when we can connect to our three intellectual powers of *Chochmah, Binah,* and *Daat,* translated as wisdom, understanding and knowledge, which are an acronym for the word *ChaBaD*. By being mindful of this while reciting and meditating on the Shema prayer, we can fill the right chamber of the heart, where our Divine soul manifests emotionally, with love, thereby creating a *dveykut* (clinging) to Hashem with the *mitzvah* out of love. This has been expanded upon by many Rabbinic sources and breaks down as a three-fold process: (1) focus meditation on the Light of Infinite, which leads to (2) emotional arousal, which leads to (3) a renewed connection and commitment to observe the *mitzvot*, all of which is spelled out in the prayer itself. Meditation: "Hear, Oh Israel, God is our God, God is One." Emotional arousal: "And you shall love God, your God." And observance of the *mitzvot*: "Bind them as a sign on your hand... Write them on the door-posts of your house, etc." This meditative-emotional arousal is also the goal of the *tefillah* that precedes the *Shema*. The Alter Rebbe explains that in this time, the *yetzer hara* that resides in the left chamber of your heart, where the animalistic soul manifests, is temporarily subdued by the good which has spread to the right chamber by the *ChaBaD* in your brain. It is in this meditation that, when focused on the Light of Infinite, we can receive the *mochin de-gadlut* of the Supernal mind.[37]

Vayehi Or: It is important to differentiate the light of the first day of creation from the light of the fourth day. On the fourth day, The Holy One creates the sun, moon and all of the luminaries of the sky. That is the light that our minds go to when we think of the word. But there is a more primordial light, which is the fabric of absolutely everything—this is the light of the first day of creation. We are all made of this light. With the exile from Gan Eden, our skin went from Or with an *alef* to Or with an *ayin*. It is our sacred task to remember this light of the first day and not to confuse it with the light of the fourth day, which simply gestures at it.

Since light is the purpose, it was created first, and all creation that came after stems from the initial intention of, "Let there be light." In that same verse it says, "and it was good". With every subsequent utterance, Hashem ends the creation with "and it was good." From this we see that the Infinite One infused light into every subsequent creation. Now we see the connection, mentioned in the Zohar, between light and hiddenness or secret. The light that was once fully revealed prior to all of creation is now hidden in this physical and material world. The more we reveal it, the closer we get to a time of full revelation and redemption, when the light is likened to that of the first day.

The Zohar teaches that every day in the year as well as every limb in the body has a spiritual counterpart. Reb Natan teaches that the three paragraphs of the Shema prayer contain 248 words, which is the *gematria* of *RaCheM* (רחם, compassion). Compassion grows from belief in Hashem and working on that connection. Since the more a person is able to live in the consciousness that we are all one, the more they will naturally feel the pain and the joy of others—delighting in their accomplishments and feeling deeply their sorrow. It is then that a person is considered a human being with 248 limbs (which correspond to the 248 "positive" *mitzvot* that require action to fulfill).[38]

Compassion is also born of pausing and not reacting at all times. We have 365 sinews which correspond to the 365 "negative" *mitzvot* that are the things we should not do, which in turn correspond to the 365 days of the year, as it is something we have to be diligent with at all times. Sinews (or nerves) through the brain instruct our limbs to act. Being mindful of Hashem's instructions of when not to act in situations where we "feel" like acting strengthens each corresponding sinew or nerve, elevating it and causing holiness to dwell upon it. On the flip side is failing to resist the temptation or to perform the *mitzvah,* which actually weakens the limb (or nerve), causing a spirit of impurity to dwell on it. And so each nerve and each day has a corresponding angelic force. Otherwise, the person is considered an animal in human form.

Chazal teach that just as there are 248 members (limbs and organs), there are 248 spiritual limbs of the soul that enliven and govern the body. The Arizal teaches that the soul of a righteous individual consists of 248 spiritual members, and each one contains a spark from some of the souls of the other righteous individuals. They are interconnected in that way. Thus all the Divine favor that the person receives is in the merit of the souls of the other righteous people who are connected and dependent on them. The Arizal explains that this is why the righteous value their possessions, since they know that they come from above. This is why Yakov went back across the river Yabok (in *parashat* Vayishlach), even though it was just a couple of small jars. By fulfilling one's mission, the righteous person is helping to complete the missions of their ancestors, and any other souls with which they share a multiple lifetime connection. It is crucial to realize that what Hashem gives isn't only to fulfill one's own mission, but that of the missions of those that came before. Thus valuing possessions is a sign of not only allowing increased revelation of the Light of Infinite in this world, but also furthering the state of completion of those souls that need it. The Arizal explains that a righteous person can't disdain the material—if nothing could be accomplished through them, Hashem wouldn't have given them. This is why Yakov returned to collect the small jars because otherwise it would appear as though he didn't value them at all. Everything given to us must be valued, and so he went back to show just that. And in this battle Yakov had with this angel 'Satan' [the Angel of Death], just as with our own struggle with the *yetzer hara*, but not on our own merits alone, but with the merits of the righteous ones that came before us and with that, we are able to overcome and outweigh the *sitra achra*. So, too, with all the good and holiness that we take on, we elevate and hopefully fulfill missions of the ones that came before us.[39]

The Rebbes

"If I am not for myself, who will be for me?" אם אין אני לי מי לי [1]

My take on this verse from Pirkei Avot is that we, as these epic beings endowed with intellect, heart, talent and creativity, need to find ways to bring our unique gifts into this world, for ourselves and to share with others. Just as no two fingerprints are alike, none of our true expressions come out in the same way as any other person.

We are meant to share our unique gifts and perspectives with the world. As I undertake creative projects, I stay inspired by so many people around me and those who have come before me, and I thought it important to highlight some of the Rebbes who have been my biggest influence, especially in my writing of these five books. So, I want to give some background on these special individuals, so that you, dear reader, can get a sense of the influence these souls have had on the following chapters.

In Chronological Order:

RASHBI, RABBI SHIMON BAR YOCHAI (135–170 CE / 80–160)

There's probably no other book, besides the Torah itself, that has inspired my writing as much as the teachings of the holy Zohar ("Brilliance"). I can still feel what it was like to be in Meron on Lag BaOmer, on the anniversary of Rabbi Shimon Bar Yochai's passing. Every year, tens of thousands of Jews visit Meron to celebrate, singing around bonfires and praying by R' Shimon's gravesite. The town is tiny, on top of a mountain, a few miles north of Tzfat and west of the Sea of Galilee. It barely has a main street, but the energy of the renowned Holy Sage breathes life into its surroundings.

R' Shimon was a 2nd century Tannaitic sage in ancient Judea. He was born in Galilee and became one of the most eminent disciples of Rabbi Akiva, whom he studied with for 13 years in Bnei Brak.

They became so close that Rabbi Akiva would call him son. This was during the persecution by the Roman Emperor Hadrian, a time when the Talmudic Academies were shut down, and the study of the Talmud was forbidden on penalty of death. Nevertheless, Rabbi Akiva continued to publicly teach the Talmud, and R' Shimon was present throughout, until the time of R' Akiva's arrest. Even this couldn't keep R' Shimon away from his teacher, so he continued to study by his side, even in prison, as R' Akiva was condemned to die a martyr's death as a Kiddush Hashem (sanctification of G-d's name).

R' Shimon went on to become one of the greatest teachers of Jewish Law and ethics. His presence in the Talmud reflects his holy character and devotion to the Torah. Talmud Berachot[2] relates that R' Shimon had previously studied at Yavne, under Gamaliel II and Yehoshua ben Hananiah. R' Shimon is most famous as the author of the sacred Zohar, a book containing mystical interpretations of the Torah, which serves as the main source of the Kabbalah ("Receiving"), the mystical branch of Judaism.

RAMBAM, RABBI MOSES BEN MAIMON (1135–1204)

Just the title to his Sefer—The Guide to the Perplexed—had me enthralled, and I've been obsessed with Rambam's writings and teachings ever since. Rabbi Moses ben Maimon, also known as Maimonides or Rambam, was born on the fourteenth day of Nissan—the day before Passover—in the year 1135, in Cordova, Spain. The most renowned of the Jewish medieval scholars, Rambam was a Talmudist, halachist, physician, and philosopher, and is one of the most important figures in the history of Torah scholarship.

Rambam was a descendent of a distinguished and scholarly family tracing its ancestry to Rabbi Yehudah HaNassi, the compiler of the Mishnah, and even further back to the royal house of King David.[3]

Rambam was one of the most prolific Rabbi's in history, writing a commentary on the Torah and the Mishnah—the compilation of the Oral Tradition of the Torah—and a book known to most by the title, *A Guide to the Perplexed.*

Rambam's father was a massive influence on him and his work, as his father served as Dayan—a judge in the Jewish court of law—of the Jewish community of Cordova and was famous for both his vast Torah knowledge, as well as his scholarship in mathematics and astronomy. He learned Scripture, Talmud, and every aspect of the Jewish religion and tradition from his father, Rabbi Maimon.

It was his father who pushed him to study philosophy and medicine, fields in which he later became world renowned. Rambam was barely Bar Mitzvah when the Almohades conquered Cordova in 1148.

As had been the case in many surrounding countries at the time, the tolerance towards Judaism was not very great and so the Muslims where Rambam lived offered the Jewish population the choice of conversion to Islam, death, or expulsion from their native land.

With the choice of either surrendering their eternal faith or their very life, or abandoning their homeland where they had lived for many centuries, leaving everything behind to seek refuge in a hostile unwelcomed world; Rambam's family, as well as a vast majority of Jews, chose exile and left Cordova. Most who did not leave either met a martyr's death, or became insincere converts to Islam, merely outwardly, all the while, secretly, in their hearts and in the privacy of their homes, observing and practicing all the elements of a life of Torah.

As the conquering Almohadian hordes swept all across Southern Spain, Rambam's family wandered about from city to city without being able to stay in any one place for a long period. After a decade of a nomadic life, they joined a group of fugitives who headed toward North Africa and eventually settled, in 1159, in Fez, then the capital of Morocco.

But they were still not destined to enjoy peace and security. After a five year stay in Fez they had to leave due to continuous religious intolerance and persecution. They made their way to Egypt, by way of Jerusalem and Chevron. Unlike other Muslim countries, the Jews in Egypt, under the tolerant rule of the Fatimide caliphs, were granted complete religious and civil freedom—while developing their religious, cultural and communal life without any restrictions. Rambam settled in 12th-century-Egypt, and his writings (in Arabic and Hebrew) spread across the Jewish world and beyond, enriching philosophy, and medicine, and becoming an indispensable part of the study of Judaism.

THE ARIZAL, RABBI YITZHAK LURIA (1534–1572)

I still remember ascending the steps towards the Ari's mikveh in Tzfat, Israel. I knew it would be cold, but was not prepared for how cold it really was. It was a shock to my system, both body and soul, but one I needed and won't soon forget, as I dipped into ritual immersion in the mystical 800 year old pool.

Rabbi Yitzhak Luria is a great Sage from the 16th century, who lived in Egypt and Tzfat, Israel. He is known as the Arizal—an acronym meaning the "lion of blessed memory"—or simply as The Ari. Lurianic Kabbalah is a system which The Ari developed out of the teachings from the Zohar. He decoded elements of the Zohar, leaving certain parts beyond comprehension for the average Torah scholar, and retaining that which only a scholar deeply versed in the "revealed Torah" could possibly understand. In essence, he revealed the depths of the "hidden Torah," also known as the Sod or secret.

Following the Jews' expulsion from Spain in 1492, a number traveled to Israel and settled in Tzfat. Other Jews went West to discover the Americas, while a good number went East to Turkey. The Ari was clearly destined for the holy, mystical city of Tzfat.

Rabbi Joseph Karo, author of the Bet Yosef, which traces the source and origin of contemporary Jewish Law, and the Shulchan Aruch, the Code of Jewish Law, was the Rabbi of the city when the Ari arrived. The city was a haven for mystics, one of whom was The Ramak (Rabbi Moses Cordevero). But it was The Arizal that was by far the most renowned Kabbalist of the day.

Though the Arizal, like Rebbe Nachman, only lived for 38 years, he revealed many of the hidden layers of the Torah, as all of its secrets were open to him.

His teachings were recorded in Kitvei Ari, the "writings of the Arizal," by his foremost disciple, Rabbi Chaim Vital, who he had met in the last two years of his life.

It's said that without the Kitvei Ari, the Zohar does not make much sense at all. It is the Ari that revealed the means to understand and digest all of the myriad layers hidden in the Zohar. Without it, the Zohar is seemingly just a collection of poetic texts.

The main work of the Kitvei Ari is the Etz Chaim (Tree of Life). For the person who has mastered its content, what was once hidden becomes revealed. His other work, the Pri Etz Chaim (Fruit of the Tree of Life) and Shaar HaKavanot (Gate of Meditations) show how to apply the various teachings of the Etz Chaim to Judaic rituals and meditation such as putting on tzitzit or tefillin, the power of prayer, and the elevation of food from the physical to the spiritual.[4]

His other work is referred to as the Shemonah Shearim (Eight

Gates). The first gate, Shaar HaHakdamot (Gate of Introductions), covers the same theoretical ground as the Etz Chaim. Then comes Shaar Maamarei Rashbi, the "Gate of Zoharic Teachings;" Shaar Maamarei Chazal, the "Gate of Talmudic Teachings;" Shaar HaPesukim, the "Gate of Biblical Verses;" Shaar HaMitzvot, the "Gate of the Commandments;" Shaar HaKavanot, the "Gate of Meditations;" Shaar Ruach HaKodesh, the "Gate of Divine Inspiration;" and the eighth and final is the Shaar HaGilgulim, the "Gate of Reincarnations." It is his seventh sefer, Shaar Ruach Hakodesh, which describes how to use the Lurianic system and is the key to the entire Kitvei Ari because it actually shows how to put the teachings into practice, whereas all the previous gates deal with theory.[5]

As stated previously, the Arizal formulated the Kabbalah into a system that is called Lurianic Kabbalah, and as Chaim Vital in the name of The Ari teaches, "It is a Mitzvah to reveal this wisdom." This is important because prior to the Arizal, the Kabbalah was held only within a close circle, the word Kabbalah means 'that which is received, or the root, Kabal, to receive.' Kabbalah was received by a very select few. But the Arizal knew the time had come for the secrets of the Kabbalah to be spread more widely, outside the inner circles to affect the spirits of the souls of the people. It is through the Arizal that the Kabbalah became popular and revolutionized the modern Judaic landscape.

THE BA'AL SHEM TOV, RABBI ISRAEL BAAL SHEM TOV (1698–1760)

The holy and revolutionary perspectives of the Baal Shem Tov, have colored my life in more ways than possibly any other Rabbi. I consider myself equal parts Chabad and Breslov, both of which would not exist without the life of this righteous figure.

The Baal Shem Tov (which literally translates as "master of the good name") and/or the acronym "Besht," is the Eastern-European 18th century mystic and founder of the chassidic movement, changed the landscape of Judaism forever.

The Baal Shem Tov breathed new life into a nation that was in need of the revitalizing spirit and light that shined forth from his stories, teachings and philosophy, which permeate almost all places and spaces in Judaism to this day. Indeed, all of Chassidut stems from the Besht.

The Baal Shem Tov's influence came forth exactly when it was needed, during the late 17th century in Europe when the Jews were still reeling from the devastation at the hands of the Khmelnitsky pogroms of 5408 and 5409 (1648–1649 CE). The massacres had left tens of thousands of Jews dead, while the devastated survivors struggled to rebuild their broken lives and communities.

In the wake of the pogroms, brief (albeit false) hope came by way of the infamous Shabtai Zvi (may his memory be erased). Shabtai Zvi was a false Messiah who led thousands of desperate Jews believing him to be the true Messiah who would redeem them and their suffering from exile. After he turned out to be a fraud, Shabtai Zvi converted to Islam under pressure from the Ottoman Turks and the Jews at the time felt the heavy weight of life under persecution. Many families were left without a livelihood, and the tradition of Torah study at a young age was soon abandoned. Only the wealthy that were few in number could afford a proper Torah education for their children. This left a generation that was ignorant, yet still devoted. This also left a rift between the scholarly and intellectually secular to the point that the two groups prayed at separate synagogues.

Meanwhile, in a small Polish town of Tloste, The Baal Shem Tov's parents, Eliezer and Sarah, lived in simple piety, serving Hashem with pure hearts. While many took Eliezer as a simpleton, he was actually a member of the group of "hidden tzaddikim," who were devoted Jews with unusual gifts who dedicated their lives to improving the plight of the Jewish people in both spiritual and material matters.

On the 18th of Elul, 5458, Eliezer and Sarah gave birth to their only child—Yisrael—the name of the Jewish People. His life and legacy was the wake-up call for those Jews that were in a deep spiritual slumber.

Fast forward to age 18, Yisrael got married and his wife died shortly after. Yisrael put his focus into teaching in the Tloste cheder. His deep insights into human nature began to spread throughout the community and he was asked to assist in civil disputes. He later moved to the town of Brody, remarried and then settled in a small village deep in the Carpathian Mountains where he spent most of his time secluded in study and meditation, a period of his life he looked back at fondly.

In the mountains, Yisrael had learned from local villagers the healing properties of various plants and herbs. He would heal a variety of bodily ailments for those who he came into contact with. His name came to be known as a Baal Shem, a healer and people from all over would come to see him. And increasingly he would begin to heal their spirit as much if not more than their physical illnesses. He taught and stressed the importance that the Torah places on optimism and joy and would encourage each person in their own service of God. It was this affectionate disposition that brought the addition of "tov" (good) to his name, becoming the Baal Shem Tov.

It's said that in 5484 (1724), on Yisrael's 26th birthday, the ancient prophet Achiya Hashiloni (who had taught Torah to Elijah the Prophet some 2,500 years earlier) appeared to him revealing the secrets of the entire Torah. The teaching began with the word

"Bereishit" (the first word of the Torah) and ending with the last words of the Torah, ten years later.

It was on his 36th birthday, after six years of pressure from his long-time mentors Rabbi Adam and Achiya Hashiloni to publicly reveal his greatness, the Baal Shem Tov began to share his Torah and healing teachings in a revealed way.

His outlook on theology and life differed from that of his peers, with a focus on purity of intent and joy and humility over scholarly achievements—something that opened the door to speak for even the simplest peasants, where they felt the power and pleasure of serving God through passionate prayer.

It was in 5500 (1740), when he felt that his following was strong enough, that he moved to what was at the time the center of Chassidism around him, to the small town of Mezhibush, where he lived out his days.

Mezhibush became home to some of the greatest Jewish minds of the time including Rabbi Yaakov Yosef of Pulnaa, Rabbi Pinchas of Koritz, and Rabbi Dovber (who would later succeed the Baal Shem Tov as the leader of the Chasidim). These students, after the Baal Shem Tov's passing, became the foremost transmitters of Chassidic thought to European Jewry as a whole.

Of course, the Baal Shem Tov's teachings weren't embraced by all, fear of the revolutionary outlook was met by staunch opposition from a good deal of traditional Talmudists who had suspicions that much like Shabti Zvi, the false messiah a century earlier, the Baal Shem Tov with his Kabbalistic undertones was hiding his true intentions to do much the same. They thought his belief that the ignorant merited glory and that the Light of Infinite permeated even the most mundane of matter, was far too unconventional to become mainstream. In time and through the generations an eventual mutual respect was fostered and an appreciation for the truth and holiness of the Baal Shem Tov's teachings came to the fore.

Through the teachings of the Baal Shem Tov, and the Rabbi's that came after, Chassidism, especially Chabad has become one of the most vibrant Jewish ways of life around the world. The Baal Shem Tov is the great-grandfather of Rebbe Nachman of Breslov, one of the other fastest growing sects of Chassidism today.

THE "ALTER REBBE," RABBI SHNEUR ZALMAN OF LIADI (1745–1812)

When I lived in Crown Heights, my soul connected to the joyous movement of Chabad and I spent many Shabbatot davening at 770 on Eastern Parkway. What I didn't get a chance to do when I lived there was dig deep into the teachings of the Tanya; something that I try and do every day now. The teachings of the Alter Rebbe keep me inspired and connected to life and light, and the following chapters would be remiss without the unique insights of the Baal HaTanya.

Rabbi Shneur Zalman of Liadi, also knows by the moniker, the "Alter Rebbe," (the older Rabbi) was a brilliant master of mysticism, philosophy, and psychology. One of the most important minds in the Chassidic movement whose slogan "G-d wants your heart" (Rachmonoh liboh boey) has filled Jewish life to this day with happiness and joy just as much for the not-yet-educated as much as the master Talmudist. The Alter Rebbe is known as the founder of Chabad Chassidism, easily one of the strongest and most dynamic branches of Chassidism.

This movement, founded in Lithuania in 5533 (1773), grew far beyond the boundaries of this once mighty center of Jewish life, and gained enthusiastic adherents throughout the world.

The Alter Rebbe is a direct descendant of the Maharal of Prague. His grandparents moved throughout Galicia and Poland, settling in Vitebsk, then a center of Torah scholarship. His father, Rabbi Baruch, moved to Liozna, near the town of Lubavitch, where Shneur Zalman was born. Lubavitch is the other name of Chabad and where the movement stems.

Shneur Zalman proved to be a brilliant mind even as a child and in order to further his development as a scholar, his father took him to a great teacher who lived in Lubavitch, by the name of Rabbi Issachar Ber of Kobilnik. In his time with Rabbi Ber, Shneur Zalman mastered the "sea of the Talmud" in all directions and began to learn Kabbalah, while in his spare time learning science and mathematics. His Rabbi soon sent word to his father that, "There is nothing more that I can teach your son; he has grown beyond me."

At 12-years old, his father took him to Vitebsk, where he was recognized as the genius that he was and seen as equal to the great scholars in the area. At 20 years of age, with his wife's consent, Shneur Zalman set out to fulfill the yearnings of his neshama at the hands of a master of such pursuits. He had two prominent centers of scholarship wanting him to join them. The first was Vilna, which is the main seat of Talmudic scholarship and was the center of the opposition to the new and rapidly growing Chassidic movement and the second, very much the opposite option—Mezeritch, the home of Rabbi Dovber, the famed Maggid of Mezeritch, whose ideology stemmed from the Baal Shem Tov and the growing Chassidic movement.

Rabbi Shneur Zalman, already a renown Torah and Talmudic scholar, realized that Vilna wouldn't quench his search and it was guidance in the service of God ("avodah") and prayer that he was needing. So Shneur Zalman headed to Mezeritch and upon meeting Rabbi Dovber and prior to being able to ask him the questions he had prepared to insure him a worthy master, Rabbi Dovber was silent and then proceeded to tell Shneur Zalman all that had been in his mind at the time and went on to answer all of the questions that he had not yet disclosed. He was of course beside himself and pleaded that he be brought into the inner circle as a student of the Maggid of Mezeritch.

As Shneur Zalman's spiritual and intellectual appetite grew, he found the Maggid's lessons on the teachings of the Baal Shem Tov to be beyond his expectations, uniting God, Israel, the Torah and the entire universe into a holy system that transcends comprehension.

At the time Rabbi Shneur Zalman wasn't recognized as a brilliant mind amongst the followers of the Maggid. That all changed when the Maggid revealed Shneur Zalman's extraordinary gifts as a "light in Israel." It was then that Rabbi Dovber instructed Rabbi Shneur Zalman, to rewrite the Code of Jewish Law, to include the latest decisions, at most 25 years old.

It had been about 200 years since Rabbi Joseph Caro had published the Shulchan Aruch, and throughout that period "Acharonim" (generations of Jewish codifiers and commentators) added to and elucidated the work of Jewish law. Once, Rabbi Shneur Zalman had completed what should have taken a lifetime, in such a short period, he was acclaimed as one of the great scholars of his time, both in the Chassidic circles and beyond.

After Rabbi Dovber passed away on Kislev 19, 5533 (1772) his disciples were tasked with spreading Chassidism, each in a different country that was assigned to them.

Rabbi Shneur Zalman was to be sent on a seemingly impossible mission, needing to spread Chassidim in Lithuania to the Misnagdim, the very opponents of Chassidism and their way of life. Shneur

Zalman was perfectly suited for such a mission, since his Talmudic scholarship was on the level of the Misnagdim which many were the top Talmudic scholars in the world at the time.

During the years he spent trying to improve the spiritual and economic conditions of Jews all over the Russo-Polish border, Rabbi Shneur Zalman developed the philosophy of Chabad Chassidism. Where each Chassid was tasked with training themselves in a life of emunah and avodat Hashem, which brings a person to the highest level of Chabad, the three intellectual powers of Chochmah, Binah, and Daat, translated as wisdom, understanding and knowledge, which are an acronym for the word ChaBaD which form a bond between the upper and lower levels, heaven and earth. This being an all encompassing dveykut (clinging) to Hashem, one of mind, heart and deed in unison, the mind understands, the heart feels and the hand performs.

His teachings are studied around the globe by countless Chassidim, friends of Chabad and intellectual spiritualists the world over. His most famous work is Likutei Amarim, better known as the Tanya, which is a mind-blowing philosophical testament to his complete mastery of both the exoteric and esoteric teachings of Torah and the great scholars that preceded him. The Alter Rebbe's understanding of the synthesis of intellect and emotion and how to bridge the two in a way to connect to the Light of Infinite, contributed to the formation of the Chabad movement, which can now be found as an elevated respite, and a home away from home for people in just about every corner of the entire world.

REBBE NACHMAN OF BRESLOV (1772–1810)

The Great-Grandson of the Baal Shem Tov, Rebbe Nachman, has changed my life and the lives of so many people I love into something transcendent. I visited his kever in Uman, Ukraine when I was in Kiev for Shabbat after playing a show in Yalta, the Black Sea, when I was there reciting Tikkun HaKlali (the complete remedy) and felt on fire for Hashem like I never had before. This was prior to my knowing about Breslov, the movement that he started and my familiarity of the rich texts of his teaching, including Likutey Moharan. My soul knew what my intellect did not yet connect, I was Breslov and these teachings were my home.

Rebbe Nachman of Breslov was born on the first of Nissan, 1772, to Feiga, daughter of Odil, daughter of the Baal Shem Tov. His father's side was also of a prominent lineage, as his father Rabbi Simcha, was the son of Rav Nachman of Horodenka, an early Chassidic leader.[6]

Rebbe Nachman was orphaned as a very young child, and spent his formative years between his uncle's house and wandering from place to place, relying on Hashem for his needs. It was then that he formed a habit of hitbodedut, the practice of secluded meditation with God where one pours out their words and heart to the Creator.

"...to establish at least an hour to be alone in a room or in the field, and to express in conversation between himself and his Maker, [including] complaints and excuses, apologies and reconciliation, and to beg him to lead him to serve Him in truth. This conversation should be in the vernacular ... in which he can best express himself and whatever lies on his heart, both regret for the past and wishes for the future ... and he should take care to accustom himself to do this every day at a set time ... and the rest of the time he should be happy."[7]

This act of speaking to the Infinite, just as one would with a friend or parent, became a hallmark of Breslov Chassidism.

At an early age, Rebbe Nachman mastered the Talmud and Jewish law at a very quick speed. But much like his great-grandfather, the

Baal Shem Tov, Rebbe Nachman associated himself with simple folk and hid his piety, this had many dismiss him and some find him to be a fool. His life was wrought with detractors and when his students would complain to him about it, he replied, "Trust me, I can make peace with the entire world and no one will disagree with me. But what can I do? There are certain spiritual chambers that can only be accessed through [overcoming] strife," citing Moshe who also faced opposition and attempts of rebellion.

Despite the great and unparalleled achievements of Rebbe Nachman, his life was full of adversity, four of his eight children died in infancy, and he lost his wife to tuberculosis, which he too would pass away from at age of 38. It was this hardship that inspired his emphasis on joy being of the utmost importance, as he would teach to others, "Struggle with all your might to be only happy at all times, since it is natural to be drawn into depression and sadness..."[8] His most famous dictum being, "Ein shum yeush ba'olam klal!", which means, "There is no such thing as despair in the world, at all!'

Rebbe Nachman's time on this earth overlapped with Rabbi Schneur Zalman of Liadi (the Alter Rebbe), who passed away two years after Rebbe Nachman. At one point, Reb Nachman wanted to have Rabbi Schneur Zalman become his foremost student, but he had his own path.

Instead he met Reb Natan on a pilgrimage to the Holy Land in 1822. Reb Natan made such a deep impression on him, that he brought him in to compile, edit, and publish his teachings in what would become Likutey Moharan and encouraged him to write his own scholarly work of Torah, the most famous of which became Likutey Halachot. Reb Natan eventually became the great leader of the Breslov movement, a testament to Rabbeinu's great wisdom and foresight.

Rebbe Nachman often hid his teachings in stories, many of which rival classic literature in both their style and lyricism. He did so, motivated by the belief that in the story form, these lessons had the power to awaken slumbering souls. These stories, which include tales of princesses and paupers, kings and knaves, sinners and saints, contain practical lessons alongside the secrets of the Torah and Kabbalah. The most famous are the Sipurei Maasiyot, which were in Hebrew and Yiddish, titled Rebbe Nachman's Stories in English, written for both the simpleton and the scholar.

The Tikkun Haklali (the complete remedy), is Rebbe Nachman's selection and order of 10 Tehillim/Psalms (16, 32, 41, 42, 59, 77, 90, 105, 137, and 150) which he described as the remedy for elevating the fallen sparks. The practice of reading Tikkun Haklali has become even more popular now then it was back then.

Most associate Rebbe Nachman with both Uman, Ukraine and the holiday of Rosh Hashanah because he would tell his followers it is important to be with him in Uman in his life and after his death during spiritually auspicious time. Rabbeinu stressed the importance to the extent that he would tell his followers, "Whether you eat or you don't eat, whether you sleep or you don't sleep, whether you daven [with proper concentration] or you don't daven—just make sure that you are with me for Rosh Hashanah!"[9] And Reb Natan was overheard saying, "Even if the road to Uman were paved with knives, I would crawl there—just to be with Rebbe Nachman for Rosh Hashanah." and also shared, "Whoever comes to Rebbe Nachman's burial place in Uman for Rosh Hashanah has a share in bringing the Redemption".[10] Uman on Rosh Hashanah is now more popular than it ever has been, attracting tens of thousands of followers of Breslov each year.[11]

The events of Rebbe Nachman, more than any other Chassidic master before him, have been carefully recorded and published in several books including *Peulat Tzadik* ("Action of the Righteous"). This glimpse into the life of the Tzadik who battled struggles both internal and external yet overcame them with an infectious joy that permeates much of Judaism today is invaluable.

In 1807, Rebbe Nachman passed through the city of Uman, stopping off at an old Jewish cemetery, telling his disciples, "This is a good place to be buried." This referencing the cemetery where thousands of Jewish martyrs of the Haidamak Massacre of Uman of 1768 were buried. He later passed away in Uman and was laid to rest in that exact spot.

His revolutionary teachings and outlook on inward enlightenment lives on to this day and as he was quoted saying, "Until the Moshiach."

REB NATAN OF BRESLOV (1780–1844)

It was years of familiarity with Rebbe Nachman's Likutey Moharan before I was properly introduced to Reb Natan's Likutey Halachot; it was from these teachings that I started to notice a shift in me. One where all the previous things I had learned had taken on new meanings, as if a new cleaner lens was placed on the seeing part of my soul. It's hard to describe the way Reb Natan articulates and expounds on the lessons of Rebbe Nachman, but the fresh perspective on always seeing the good within oneself and others, knowing that just like the moon waxes and wanes, so to do the hardships in all our lives and we have to lead with compassion and love if we hope to live a fulfilled life of happiness and connection.

Reb Natan Sternhartz was born in Nemirov, on 15 Shevat, 5540 (January 22, 1780). At thirteen, he married Esther Shaindel, the daughter of Rabbi Dovid Zvi Orbach, a prominent halachic authority in Poland and the Ukraine. At 22, Reb Natan became Rebbe

Nachman's loyal follower and developed into his the Rebbe's scribe, writing down every teaching and conversation, so close was this relationship built on revealing the hidden Torah that Rebbe Nachman said: "Were it not for Reb Natan, not a page of my writings would have remained."[12]

Reb Natan didn't meet Rebbe Nachman until he was 22. Reb Natan was already a first-rate Torah prodigy and had a career as the Rabbinical leader of many communities laid out for him; he was already a giant scholar at the time. Once he met his Rabbeinu, however, he understood that Reb Nachman was the true tzaddik and wanted nothing other than to learn from his Torah and disseminate it to the world. Even though his family didn't understand or support it at the time, Reb Natan gave up all that was waiting for him and nullified himself completely to Reb Nachman. He became a perfect reflection of Rebbe Nachman's teachings, just as the moon reflects the light of the sun and Yehoshua the light of Moshe. This is apparent in Reb Natan's illuminations in the final lesson taught by Reb Natan, which is found in hilchot Rosh Chodesh 7, which deals with the perfection of the blemish of the moon and its connection to the core teachings of Breslov, the Azamra.

After Rebbe Nachman passed away, Reb Natan moved to Breslov (1811), after Rebbe Nachman passed away and printed all of Rebbe Nachman's writings, this included the beloved Likutey Moharan. Under the strong encouragement of Rebbe Nachman, Reb Natan wrote and published his own original discourses and teachings, including Likutey Halachot. During this period, he traveled throughout the Ukraine, visiting Rebbe Nachman's followers and continuing to spread the Rebbe's teachings.

In 1822, he made his pilgrimage to Israel, an adventure with many surprises. Around this time, Reb Natan fell into poverty. Eight years later, the number of followers going to Uman for Rosh Hashanah increased and Reb Natan oversaw the construction of a large Breslov synagogue.

In late 1834, there was a movement fueled by fierce opposition to Reb Natan and the Breslover Chassidim. The opposition led to Reb Natan's temporary imprisonment by the authorities. After he was released, Reb Natan fled from city to city in the Ukraine, only returning to Breslov a year later. Shortly after he was banned from the town of Breslov, and was under court order to remain in the city of his birth. Though he was able with permission to travel to Uman for Rosh Hashanah and for other select occasions. With those few exceptions, he was essentially restricted to the town of Nemirov. This only increased the opposition's ability to try and ruin his name and movement. With the leader of the movements sudden death in 1838, the opposition died down and Reb Natan returned to Breslov.

Despite the great personal suffering he was dealt from both poverty and opposition, Reb Natan was single handedly responsible for shaping the Breslov movement into the vibrant force it is today. Reb Natan had five sons and one daughter.[13]

On the morning of his passing, 10 Tevet, 5605 (December 20, 1844), Reb Natan had the first two stories of Rabbi Nachman's stories read to him. The second story ends, "…let us go home!" Hearing these words, Reb Natan nodded his head as if to say, "Yes, it is my time to go home." He passed away later that day in his home in Breslov, just before Shabbat.[14]

THE LUBAVITCHER REBBE, RABBI MENACHEM MENDEL SCHNEERSON (1902–1994)

I can't think of a more impactful and influential leader of the last hundred + years than The Lubavitcher Rebbe, Rabbi Menachem

Mendel Schneerson, of righteous memory. There is hardly a corner of the globe that you can find yourself in that doesn't include a Chabad house where you will be greeted with a smile and some warm food by a Rabbi and his wife and family, who continue to be inspired by the teachings of The Rebbe. The Rebbe believed in shining light on the soul; spirituality and oneness over physicality and separation. That which divides us conceals Hashem, and The Rebbe was about revelation.

When I was married, I lived in Crown Heights, Brooklyn and our chuppah was at the world headquarters of Chabad, 770 Eastern Parkway or simply known around the world as 770. There are replicas of the building in different cities around the world. As I walked in circles, I felt the weight of what The Rebbe brought down to this life and when it came time for the tradition of going into the Yichud room, we were escorted into The Rebbe's study and his kitel was placed upon my shoulders, little did I know at the time, The Rebbe would change my outlook and mission in life for the good and forever. There is never a week that goes by without my being inspired by a teaching of the Rebbe, generally in Likuttei Sichot, and I quote many of his insights from the *Parashah* in my writing.

The seventh leader in the Chabad-Lubavitch dynasty, The Rebbe who was named after his ancestor, the third Chabad Rebbe, Rabbi Menachem Mendel of Lubavitch, has changed the lives of hundreds of thousands of followers and millions of admirers around the world, he may very well be the one individual more than any other of the last thousand years responsible for stirring the conscience and spiritual awakening of world Jewry.

The Rebbe was born in 1902, on the 11th day of Nissan, in Nikolaev, Russia, to the Talmudic scholar, kabbalist, and leader Rabbi Levi Yitzchak and Rebbetzin Chana Schneerson. Rebbetzin Chana (1880–1964) was known for her loving-kindness and courage which became apparent when her husband's exile by the Soviets to a remote village in Asian Russia, and she began to labor to make inks from herbs she gathered in the fields so that her husband Rabbi Levi Yitzchak could continue writing his commentary on kabbalah and other Torah subjects.

When the Rebbe was nine years old, he dove into the Black Sea to save the life of a little boy who had rowed out to sea and lost control of his small boat. That innate feeling of being responsible for all those around him was a big part of his mission from an early age. This awareness and occupation with those "in danger" has dominated his teaching, writing and way of life throughout his days and the days of all his followers, whether it be Jews in isolated communities, in dire straits, and those under repressive regimes, The Rebbe viewed every person as an integral part of the whole that made up the body of the Jewish nation.

The Rebbe was already considered a Torah prodigy by the time he reached his Bar Mitzvah and spent his teen years immersed in the study of Torah.

In 1928, he married the sixth Rebbe's daughter, Rebbetzin Chaya Mushka, in Warsaw. She was the Rebbe's life partner for sixty years and passed away on 22 Sh'vat in 1988.

The Rebbe studied in the University of Berlin and at the Sorbonne in Paris where it was most likely that he mastered mathematics and the sciences. Having been rescued from the Holocaust, the Rebbe and the Rebbetzin arrived in the United States on Monday, Sivan 28, 5701 (June 23, 1941).

Without losing a beat in America, The Rebbe began disseminating Torah and Judaism and Chassidic teachings through the establishment of three Lubavitch organizations under the Rebbe's leadership:

Merkos L'Inyonei Chinuch ("Central Organization For Jewish Education"), Kehot Publication Society, and Machne Israel, a social services agency.[15]

With his father-in-law's encouragement, the Rebbe began publishing his notations to various Chassidic, Kabbalistic, and a wide range of responses on Torah subjects. As soon as his work was published and disseminated, his brilliant mind was recognized around the world.

It was with reluctance that the Rebbe ascended to leadership of the Lubavitch movement, after the passing of his father-in-law, Rabbi Yosef Yitzchak Schneersohn, in 1950. As so many have come into contact with, Lubavitch centers and Chabad Houses, with its outreach philosophy, soon started to spring up in dozens of cities and university campuses around the world.

The Rebbe understood that every good deed brings another in its wake and that with every effort of outreach, humanity comes that much closer to its ultimate goal, the time of universal awareness of G-d, known as the time of Moshiach. The Rebbe spread the message that the time is imminent and that every one of us has the power to actualize the redemption by increasing in acts of loving-kindness.

It was on Monday afternoon (March 2, 1992), while praying at the gravesite of his father-in-law, that the Rebbe suffered a physical blow, a stroke that paralyzed his right side and hindered his ability to speak. Two years and three months later, the Rebbe passed away on the 3rd of Tammuz, 5754 (June, 12 1994).

The Rebbe remains the most universally recognized and celebrated figure of the last hundred years from a Chassidic dynasty. His outreach, wisdom and mission lives on through all that came into contact with him, and all that continue to spread Torah in the loving and inclusive way in which he pioneered.

The Rebbe led by example, of abilities we all have and the urgency that we need to feel in order to actualize our potential and shine a light unto one another in order to usher in the final redemption, may it come speedily in our days!

ABRAHAM JOSHUA HESCHEL (1907–1972)

When I was a teenager, my dad would lovingly talk to me about Abraham Joshua Heschel. He first went to hear Heschel's public lectures when he was in undergraduate school at Northern Illinois University, starting in the middle to late 1960s. And then attended the Jewish Theological Seminary of America (JTS), often praying close by Heschel whenever possible. As a matter of fact, Heschel sat on my dad's entrance interview committee, asking him "how do you know so much, if you did not go to yeshiva or day school?" His life was immediately changed when he read the book, *The Sabbath*. When I began to read his books, *God in Search of Man*, *Man Is Not Alone*, and his most popular, *The Sabbath*, just like my dad, I was hooked. It was as if I was reading a theological and philosophical work of dense beauty written by Dostoevsky, every line a poem onto itself, and each paragraph a manifesto to be contemplated, lived in, surrendered to.

Abraham Joshua Heschel was a spiritual radical—a Rabbi, scholar, theologian, and philosopher who was very active in the U.S. Civil Rights Movement. Considered "one of the truly great men" of his day and a "great prophet" by Martin Luther King, Jr., Heschel made it a point when speaking to Jewish Americans and African Americans that they had a responsibility for each other's liberation and for the plight of all suffering fellow humans around the world.[16]

Heschel was born in 1907 in Warsaw, Poland, to Rabbi Moshe Mordecai and Reizel Perlow Heschel and came from a long line of Chassidic Rabbis, a Polish-born Jew descending on his father's side from Dov Baer (the Maggid) of Mezeritch and Abraham Joshua Heschel of Apta (Opatow), on his mother's side from Levi Isaac of Berdichev.

At the age of 20, he enrolled in the University of Berlin. He received his PhD from the University of Berlin (1933), as well as a Rabbinic ordination from the Hochschule für die Wissenschaft des Judentums (1934) where he taught Talmud.[17]

In 1937, Martin Buber appointed him his successor as the director of the Central Organization for Jewish Adult Education in Frankfurt, Germany (Mittelstelle fuer juedische Erwachsenenbildung) and the Juedisches Lehrhaus at Frankfurt on the Main. Where he remained until his deportation to Poland by the Nazis in October of 1938 where he taught for eight months at the Warsaw Institute of Jewish Studies. He then immigrated to England where he established the Institute for Jewish Learning in London.

He immigrated to America in 1940 by invitation from Julian Morgenstern to teach at Hebrew Union College in Cincinnati, where he was associate professor of philosophy and Rabbinics for five years. It was in this time that Heschel quickly became a leading public intellectual and civil rights crusader, best known for marching and championing for civil rights alongside Martin Luther King Jr. in Selma, Alabama and beyond.

In 1945, he became professor of Jewish ethics and mysticism at New York's Jewish Theological Seminary of America (JTS), a post he held for the rest of his life. In 1946 he married Sylvia Strauss, who birthed their only child, Susannah Heschel.

Heschel's books and studies focused on medieval Jewish philosophy—on Saadiah Gaon, Solomon ibn Gabirol, Maimonides, and Don Isaac Abrabanel—as well as on Chasidism and Kabbalah. He was admired as one of the most influential modern philosophers of religion in the United States, where his work is widely recognized and celebrated in both Jewish and Christian circles.

Martin Luther King would say of Heschel that he, "is one of the persons who is relevant at all times, always standing with prophetic insights" to guide persons with a social consciousness.[18] Both men were driven by the notion of a collective responsibility for the fate of all mankind and believed that the struggle to overcome injustice must be universal.[19]

RABBI SHLOMO CARLEBACH (1925–1994)

It's difficult to think of a single person who hasn't in some way come into contact with a beautiful niggun (devotional melody) of Shlomo Carlebach. More than any other Rabbi, Carlebach composed melodies to the tefillot (prayers) that are sung all over the world by Jews from all denominations. You could say that he created a new Chassidic musical genre. Many synagogues in Israel and the States have Shabbat melodies that are almost exclusively Carlebach. When I lived in Israel attending Yeshiva in Bait Vagan and Maalot Dafna, I would often go to Moshav Modi'in, also known as the Carlebach Moshav. The entire Shabbat would be sublime, something not of this world—the spiritual energy, the melodies and Havdalah with all the families gathering around the fire, wine, and incense singing the Shabbat out, sanctifying and distinguishing between the holy and the mundane. The music that grew out of the Moshav and Carelebach, including Ben Zion Solomon and sons and the Moshav band continue to inspire young generations in ways that transcend words.

Shlomo Carlebach was born in Berlin in 1925 and is a descendant of a Rabbinical dynasty in pre-Holocaust Germany. Growing up in Baden near Vienna, his father, Rabbi Naphtali Carlebach, served as Chief Rabbi (1931–1938). The Carlebach family traveled to Lithuania in hopes of safety, with the rise of Nazism, eventually immigrating to New York where Shlomo's father became the Rabbi of Congregation Kehilath Jacob on New York City's Upper West Side.

Shlomo and his twin brother Eli Chaim studied at Mesivta Torah Vodaas, a Charedi Yeshiva high school in Williamsburg until April 1943. They teamed up with a dozen students to help Rabbi Aharon Kotler establish the first Charedi full time Torah learning Kollel in Lakewood, New Jersey.

In 1949, Shlomo left Lakewood to begin a long lasting and deeply impactful career traveling as an outreach emissary of the Lubavitcher Rebbe, Rabbi Menachem Mendel Schneerson, disseminating the message of Chassidic Judaism in America.

In 1954, Shlomo received Rabbinic ordination from Rabbi Yitzhak Hutner, the Rosh Yeshiva of Chaim Berlin Yeshiva in Brooklyn.

Rabbi Shlomo Carlebach is regarded as one of the most influential composers of Jewish religious music of the 20th century and a pioneer of the modern neo-Hasidic renaissance. He revolutionized zemirot (Jewish sacred songs), transforming synagogue services throughout the world.

In the aftermath of the Holocaust, Reb Shlomo revived the Jewish spirit, helping thousands of disenchanted youths re-embrace their rich and beautiful heritage.

His teachings, songs, and stories weaved a tapestry and new form of heartfelt, soulful Judaism—one that was filled with a love for all human beings. In the tradition of the Baal Shem Tov and Rebbe Nachman, Shlomo discovered and uncovered the good in every person, found holiness in the outcasts, treasures in the beggars, and righteousness in the rebels.

His first record in 1959 was titled, "Songs of My Soul," and his third record, "At the Village Gate" was produced by Vanguard Records in 1963, and marked the first time that a religious Jewish artist produced an album with a major American record company.

He founded a commune-like synagogue called The House of Love and Prayer. "If I would have called it Temple Israel, nobody would have come," he said. "I had the privilege of reaching thousands of kids. Hopefully, I put a little seed in their hearts."

"Holy brothers and sisters, I have something really deep to tell you," was his way of addressing a crowd. He would see the "pintele Yid" (i.e. that no matter how distant one may become, there is always a Jewish point deep within, some small spark waiting to be ignited with wholeness and holiness) in every one.

In 1975, Reb Shlomo closed The House of Love and Prayer and took the remnants of his congregation to Israel, where he established the small settlement of Moshav Me'or Modi'in, near Ben Gurion Airport.

Rabbi Shlomo Carlebach died of a heart attack on a flight to Canada in 1994 (the 16th of Cheshvan 5755). He is buried in Israel at Har HaMenuchot. At the time of his death, Rabbi Carlebach had become a legend of sorts, having had a career that spanned 40 years in which he composed thousands of melodies and recorded 27 albums which continue to have widespread popularity and appeal. His influence continues to this day in "Carlebach minyanim" and at Jewish religious gatherings in many cities and remote areas around the globe.[20]

RABBI ARYEH KAPLAN (1934–1983)

In high school, I began reading anything Rabbi Aryeh Kaplan wrote, and he wrote a lot, just as many books as his years on this planet, 48 titles. I continued to read his writing throughout college, going to the same university as him, University of Maryland, where he earned his M.S. degree in Physics. His writing spanned Judaic thought, from Jewish meditation to the his mystical and academic translation of the esoteric *Sefer Yetzirah: The Book of Creation* and *The Bahir* to revealing the hidden secrets of our ancient rituals in books written as a sort of introductory pamphlet on Jewish beliefs and philosophy, which were written at the request of NCSY, which include, *Tefillin, Waters of Eden: The Mystery of the Mikvah, Tzitzith: A Thread of Light*, and *Sabbath: Day of Eternity*. I remember reading the weekly Parashah from his translation, *The Living Torah* and if that weren't enough, Rabbi Kaplan was the primary translator of the "Torah Anthology," a 45-volume translation of Me'am Lo'ez from Ladino (Judæo-Spanish) into English.

Aryeh Kaplan was born in the Bronx, New York City to a Sefardi Recanati family from Salonika, Greece. His mother, Fannie Kaplan, died on December 31, 1947, when he was 13, and his two younger sisters, Sandra and Barbara, were sent to a foster home. Kaplan was expelled from public school after acting out, leading him to grow up as a "street kid" in the Bronx.

Kaplan did not grow up religious and his family had only a slight connection to Jewish practice, but he was encouraged to say Kaddish for his mother after her passing. On his first day at the minyan, Henoch Rosenberg, a 14-year Klausenburger Chassid, realized that young Aryeh was out of place, as he was not wearing tefillin or opening a siddur, and befriended him. Rosenberg and his siblings taught Kaplan Hebrew, and within a few days, Kaplan was learning Chumash.

When he was 15, Kaplan enrolled at Yeshiva Torah Vodaas, and at age 18 was among "a small cadre of talmidim" selected to help Rabbi Simcha Wasserman open Yeshiva Ohr Elchonon, a new yeshiva in Los Angeles.

Kaplan then studied at the Mir Yeshiva in Jerusalem in Israel, where he received Rabbinic ordination from some of Israel's foremost Rabbinic authorities, including Yoreh Yoreh from Rabbi Yitzhak HaLevi Herzog and Yadin Yadin from Rabbi Eliezer Yehuda Finkel in 1956.[21]

It is this drastic shift in this upbringing and revelatory epiphanies throughout his teenage years that contributed to Kaplan being highly regarded as a significant factor in the growth of the baal *teshuvah* movement.

I didn't realize how much of an influence Rebbe Nachman's work was on Rabbi Kaplan until I read, *Until the Mashiach: The Life of Rabbi Nachman*, *Rabbi Nachman's Stories* and the incredible, *Outpouring of the Soul Rabbi Nachman's Path in Meditation*, this book was published by Chaim Kramer and his publishing company, Breslov Research Institute, Rav Kramer has been a major influence on me with his own books and translation of Likutey Moharan, largely responsible for disseminating Breslov teaching, I was honored to have him present at the Light of Infinite festival. When I discovered that he had worked with Rabbi Kaplan, my interest in him and his work grew even greater.

Rabbi Aryeh Kaplan was born in 1934, and passed away 48 years later, on the 14th of Shevat.[22]

RABBI LORD JONATHAN SACKS (1948–2020)

Rabbi Lord Jonathan Sacks' writing always reminded me of Abraham Joshua Heschel, they both had a way of relating the esoteric and mystical in a universal fashion, poetic and poignant. His books inspired the promise of redemption and the love that religion could bring about. I think everyone should read *The Dignity of Difference* and the Biblically curious should keep up with this "Covenant and Conversations" series. I always found meaning in reading the intro sections to the holiday Machzors that he would publish with Koren publishing, the typography was slick and his introduction to both the Machzor itself and the rituals and import of the Chaggim were deep and profound, just the mindset needed to enter into the High Holidays.

An international religious leader, philosopher, award-winning author, Rabbi Sacks was very unique, no other Rabbi that I know of has been knighted by Her Majesty The Queen, as he was in 2005, being made a Life Peer, and taking his seat in the House of Lords in October 2009. Sacks was awarded the 2016 Templeton Prize in recognition of his "exceptional contributions to affirming life's spiritual dimension."[23] Described by H.R.H. The Prince of Wales as "a light unto this nation" and by former British Prime Minister Tony Blair as "an intellectual giant."[24]

Sacks was largely celebrated and recognized in his day, I heard him speak in Los Angeles and hearing his story, the son of a Polish-born Textile trader, growing up in London's East End where he didn't receive a Jewish education, instead attending a local state-funded grammar school and studying philosophy at Cambridge. Only after graduating, did he begin his Rabbinical education and joined a Yeshiva.

Sacks went on to serve as the Chief Rabbi of the United Hebrew Congregations of the Commonwealth for 22 years, between 1991 and 2013. He then went on to a number of professorships at several academic institutions including Yeshiva University, New York University and King's College London. Much like Heschel, Sacks was celebrated by Theologians and religions beyond Judaism, and was awarded 18 honorary doctorates including a Doctor of Divinity conferred to mark his first ten years in office as Chief Rabbi, by the then Archbishop of Canterbury, Lord Carey.[25]

Rabbi Sacks authored over 35 books and his 2017 TED Conference talk, viewed millions of times, was listed by TED's founder and curator Chris Anderson as one of the top ten talks of that year.[26]

Rabbi Sacks passed away at age 72, on November 7th 2020. His legacy is as one of the greatest Jewish thinkers of the 20th century; one who bridged the religious and secular world through his writing, teaching and the exemplary way in which he spent his time with us on this planet.

In Honor of
Kalonymous Dovid
ben Yitzchak HaKohen

Dedicated by
Yitzy Katz

In Loving Memory of
Arie Feder

Dedicated by
his grandson
Brandon Feder

Acknowledgements

I would love to be able to list every beautiful soul who believed in this project, and thank each person from the bottom of my heart (and I have in my previous books), but I must submit this book to Maggie McLaughlin for layout. That said, thank you to the following folks for their support: Alter Deitsch, Bracha Schoonover (in memory of David Ben Moshe Z"L), Chana Vered, Chaya Glaser, Dalia Brunschwig, David & Leah Ben Yehuda, Eli Deutsch, Ellie Bass, Eliyahu Krause, Esther Lamm, Brandon Feder, Jonah Simcha Chaim Muskat-Brown, Jordana Baruchov, Joshie Engelson, Kalman Gavriel Delmoor, Kayla Rosen, Kochava Leah DiBiase (in memory of Tikvah Hadas bat Avraham), Lauren Miryam Rachel, Marina Zilbergerts, Michael Dear, Moshe Fhima, Moshe & Chaya Nourafchan, Orel Shokri, Rabbi Harry Rozenberg, Rav Moshe Pinto, Rebbetzin Bat-Chen Grossman, Sarrit & Yossi Kovacs, Shira Jacobson, Shlomo Godsi, Simon Zipor, Teli Esther Michaan, Yaakov Bekhor (in memory of Yaakov ben Shlomo), Yermi Kurkus, Yitzchak Meir, Yitzy Katz, Yonatan Gordon & so many more!

Notes and Sources

A Special Thanks
1. Exodus 24:12
2. The Commentary of Rabbi Shlomo Carlebach, Exodus, p. 342-345

Introduction
1. Exodus 24:7
2. *Doing or Understanding – Which Comes First? by Rabbi Nissan Dovid Dubov*
3. *Zohar 1, 24a; 2, 60a*

How to Exist in Love: Tending to the Spirit
1. Likutei Moharan 1:64
2. Pirkei Avot 4:2
3. Orach Chaim 60:4
4. Isaiah 40:5
5. Arizal, Apples from the Orchard p. 241
6. Talmud Sanhedrin 37b
7. Genesis 18:27
8. Likkutei Dibburim by the Frierdiker Rebbe
9. Psalms 37:10
10. Likutei Halachot, Shomer Sakhir 2:10
11. Etz Chaim
12. Genesis 42:9
13. Likutei Halachot I, p38a-76
14. Deuteronomy 16:20
15. Talmud Makkot 10b
16. Zohar II, 182a-b
17. Bereishit Rabbah 4:6. Cf. Zohar, Part I, 46a
18. Talmud, Pesachim 66b
19. Tanya, Likkutei Amarim, ch. 12
20. Rashi; Midrash Rabbah, Numbers 16:4
21. *Likutey Moharan, Lesson 277*
22. *Talmud Berachot 17a*
23. *Proverbs 25:21*
24. *Proverbs 26:27*
25. *Likutey Moharan # 277, by Rebbe Nachman, p.355*

26. *Ecclesiastes 3:15*
27. *Maimonides, Mishneh Torah, citing "the early sages." This exact language is found in the Zohar on Genesis 2:16*
28. *Tanya, Iggeret HaKodesh, epistle 25*
29. *Igrot Kodesh, letter 6670*
30. *Likutei Moharan I 36:6*
31. *Psalms 51:17*
32. *Ibid 19:15 and Berakhot 4b:14*
33. *Numbers 22:6*
34. *Leviticus 19:18*
35. *Deuteronomy 6:5*
36. Rabbi Lord Jonathan Sacks, "How we can face the future without fear, together", TED2017

Spiritualize Reality (Vayikra)
1. Apples from the Orchard, The Arizal, p. 519
2. Leviticus 1:2
3. Psalms 51:18,19
4. Covenant and Conversation: Leviticus by Rabbi Lord Jonathan Sacks, p. 5
5. Zohar III:39a
6. Ibid Part II, 239a; Part III, 26b
7. Rebbe Nachman's Torah, compiled by Chaim Kramer, p. 303
8. Leviticus 6:18
9. Menachot 110a:13
10. Leviticus 1:2
11. Darash Moshe, p. 168
12. Leviticus 1:2
13. Talmud Sotah 3a
14. Ibid I, pp. 39a, 78
15. Ibid I, p. 163a
16. Likutey Halachot I, p. 3a
17. Deuteronomy 6:5
18. Zohar II:184a
19. Ibid II:163a

When the Screens of Separation Fall (Tzav)
1. Rav Kook Notebook 3:329
2. Rabbi Sanford Shudnow
3. Zohar I, p. 216b
4. Rav Kook Notebook 6:21
5. Tanya, Likkutei Amarim, The Alter Rebbe, lesson 32
6. Leviticus 6:10
7. Ibid 12:15
8. Talmud Berachot, 17a
9. Likutei Moharan I, 23:1
10. Proverbs 20:27
11. Deuteronomy, Rashi 16:3
12. Genesis 4:7
13. Talmud Kiddushin 49b
14. Likutei Moharan I, 33:4
15. Deuteronomy 23:8
16. "Leshuv Habaita," a song by Ishay Ribo
17. Vayikra 7:12
18. Vayikra Rabbah 9:7
19. Likutey Moharan II, 2:1
20. Likutei Halachot II, p. 288
21. Psalms 56:13
22. Likutei Halachot I. 238-120a

Step in Rhythm, Grow in Concert (Shemini)
1. Leviticus 9:1-24
2. Talmud Shabbat 10b
3. Talmud Arachim 13b
4. Likkutei Sichot, by the Lubavitcher Rebbe, Shemini, vol. 3
5. Leviticus 23:10–16
6. Exodus 1.1
7. Likutei Moharan II, 73
8. Likutey Etzot, by Rebbe Nachman, Teshuvah # 31
9. Talmud Sotah 21a
10. Likutey Moharan 4:8
11. Deuteronomy 30:14
12. Exodus 19:20
13. Malachi 3:7
14. Talmud, Berachot 26b. Zohar III, 28b
15. Torah Ohr 62b. Kuntres Ha'Avodah, p. 10
16. Leviticus 11:44
17. Yoma 39a

18. Pesachim 50b
19. Chatam Sofer 24, ד"ה והתקדשתם

Becoming a Semblance of God (Tazria)
1. Leviticus 12:3
2. Ibid 19:2
3. Tanya, Likkutei Amarim
4. I Samuel 17:8
5. Exodus 15:3
6. I Samuel 17:12
7. Talmud Sotah 42b
8. Rashi on Genesis 2:23
9. Hosea 2:25
10. Malachi 3:12
11. An Anthology of Talks, Likkutei Sichos p. 83-85
12. Leviticus 14:1
13. Leviticus 12:7
14. Leviticus 29:31
15. Genesis 17:10-11
16. Menahot 43b
17. Torat Moshe ד"ה דרש
18. R' Aryeh Kaplan, "Inner Space", p. 76
19. A Treasury of Chassidic Tales on the Torah p. 341-343
20. Sanhedrin 37b
21. Genesis 18:27

Birds in a Trap (Metzora
1. *Talmud Sukkah 5b*
2. *Zohar Vol. II, 277b*
3. *Rav Kook, Orot Hakodesh, Chapter 1*
4. *Likkutei Dibburim by the Frierdiker Rebbe*
5. *Leviticus 14:4*
6. *Talmud Arachin 15b*
7. *Vayikra Rabbah 16:7*
8. *Mishlei 18:21*
9. *Talmud Yoma 9b*
10. *Gossip – Ten Pathways to Eliminate It From Your Life and Transform Your Soul* by Lori Palatnik and Bob Burg
11. *Mishna 19*
12. *Drashot of the Ben Ish Hai Halachot p. 193*

13. *Midrash Rabbah 16:2*
14. *Psalms 34:13-14*
15. *Likutey Moharan I, 3*
16. *Zohar III, 53b*
17. *Isaiah 1:1*
18. *I Samuel 10:5*
19. *2 Kings 3:1*
20. *Zohar I, 217b*
21. *Ecclesiastes 9:12*
22. *Psalms 119:62*
23. *Psalms 57:9*
24. *Likutey Moharan #282*

G.O.A.T. amongst goats (Acharei Mot)
1. Levitikus 16:1
2. *Or HaChayim in his commentary on the beginning of Acharei Mot*
3. *Shulchan Aruch HaRav , the conclusion of section 98*
4. *Pirkei Avot 4*
5. *An Anthology of Talks, Likkutei Sichos p. 98*
6. *Talmud Pesachim 22b*
7. *Leviticus 16:7-10*
8. *Jeremiah 2:19*
9. *Leviticus 16:21-22*
10. *Talmud Yoma 62a*
11. *Likutey Halachot I p. 194*
12. *Likutey Halachot IV, p. 416*
13. *Likutey Moharan I, 109:1*
14. *Talmud Yoma 86b*
15. *'ESP" song by N.E.R.D*

Cheat Codes to Holiness (Kedoshim)s
1. Talmud Yoma 39a
2. *Talmud Avot 4:21*
3. *Man in Search of God* by Abraham Joshua Heschel, pp. 162-163
4. *LIFE* magazine 2 May 1955
5. Leviticus 19:2
6. Pirkei Avot 4:8
7. Chatam Sofer 44, ד"ה קדושי
8. Leviticus 19:13
9. Likutey Halachot I, p. 466
10. Talmud Makot 10a
11. An Anthology of Talks, Likkutei Sichos p. 154

12. Rashi on Leviticus 19:2:2
13. Leviticus 19:2
14. Chatam Sofer 44,כי ד"ה
15. Exodus 19:3-6
16. Isaiah 49:6
17. Proverbs 20:27
18. Psalms 63:9
19. The Path of the Just by Moshe Chayim Luzzatto, p. 329
20. Pirkei Avot 4:1
21. Genesis 1
22. Talmud Terumah 16a
23. Sefer Hasichot 5700, p. 115
24. Talmud Avot 2:2
25. An Anthology of Talks, Likkutei Sichos p. 146
26. Leviticus 19:18
27. Apples from the Orchard, teachings of The Arizal
28. Vayikra 19:2
29. Ibid 19:3
30. Berakhot 28a

Finding Grace in Time (Emor)
1. Zohar Hachadash, Yitro 31a; Ohr Hachayim, Shemot 3:8
2. Ohr Hachayim, Shemot 3:8
3. Talmud Taanit 8a
4. Poem by Erez Safar
5. Talmud Menachot 65b
6. Leviticus 23:15-16
7. Ibid 23:3
8. Tikuney Zohar 42 (82a)
9. Zohar 1:20a; Etz Chaim 1:4; Nefesh HaChaim 1:5; Tanya 51
10. Psalms 104:3-4
11. R' Aryeh Kaplan, "Inner Space", p. 21-22
12. R. Wisnefsky
13. The Sabbath, by Abraham Joshua Heschel
14. II Melachim 7:9 and II Devrei HaYamim 23:4,8
15. II Melachim 7:9 and II Devrei HaYamim 23:4,8
16. Leviticus 23:2
17. Ibid 23:3

18. Ibid 23:4
19. Rosh Hashanah 24a
20. Yehoshua 1:8
21. Exodus 23:16
22. Ibid 34:22
23. Numbers 16:9

All Reap, No Sow (Behar)
1. Vayikra 25:3,4
2. Ibid 25:8
3. Ibid 25:10
4. Likutey Halachot VIII, 9 62b,-63a
5. Leviticus 25:6-7
6. Chatam Sofer 67, ד"ה וידבר
7. Exodus 3:5
8. Apples from the Orchard, The Arizal
9. Exodus 19:13
10. Torat Moshe 102, ד"ה וידבר
11. Psalms 72:16
12. "Bring Back The Sabbath" by Judith Shulevitz, NYT Magazine, Jan 2, 2003
13. Rabbi Nina Beth Cardin, The Narrative of Shemittah
14. Vayikra 25:21

Faith Fuels the Future, Fear Stirs the Past (Bechukotai)
1. Jon Batiste, Grammy 2022 speech for "Best Album"
2. "Moments" song by Nas
3. "Die Hard" song by Kendrick Lamar
4. Leviticus 26:3
5. Doing or Understanding – Which Comes First? by Rabbi Nissan Dovid Dubov
6. Zohar 1, 24a; 2, 60a
7. Likuttei Halachot V, p. 426
8. Leviticus 26:14-16
9. Proverbs 27:19
10. Likkutei Torah, Bechukotai p. 48b
11. Zohar I:21a, Tikkunei Zohar 22:63b, Tanya ch. 26
12. Judges 5:31
13. An Anthology of Talks, Likkutei Sichos p. 209-211

Key Kabbalistic Concepts
1. Pirkei Avot 1:1
2. Eitz Chaim 1:1
3. Proverbs 11:24
4. Sha'arei Ha-Ledushah 3:2
5. Zohar Hachadash, Yitro 31a; Ohr Hachayim, Shemot 3:8
6. Ohr Hachayim, Shemot 3:8
7. Talmud Taanit 8a
8. Isaiah 57:16
9. Job 31:2
10. Tanya, Chapter 1, p. 45
11. Psalms 42:3
12. Ecclesiastes 7:1
13. Etz Chaim 49:3
14. Zohar 3, 41b
15. Ecclesiastes 1:14
16. Tikunei Zohar 17a
17. Psalms 89:3
18. Genesis 1:1-2
19. Bahir 2
20. Innerspace, by Aryeh Kaplan, p. 82
21. Talmud Sanhedrin 11a
22. Tur, Orach Chaim 5
23. The Living Torah on Exodus 3:15
24. Daniel 7:9
25. Exodus 25:8
26. (Song of Songs 6:3)
27. Joshua 1:8
28. Likutei Moharan I, 54:3
29. Deuteronomy 6:4-9
30. Zohar II 161b
31. Likutey Moharan I, 36:3
32. Deuteronomy 6:5
33. Song of Songs 2:5
34. Deuteronomy 6:6
35. Genesis 46:27
36. Likutei Moharan I, 36:3
37. The Practical Tanya, The Book of the Inbetweeners, Chapter 12, pp 140,141
38. Likutey Halachot I, p. 314
39. Apples from the Orchard, p. 186,187

The Rebbes
1. Pirkei Avot 1:14
2. Talmud Berachot 2 28a

3. "Maimonides: His Life and Works",
   by Dovid Zaklikowski, chabad.org
4. The Arizal By Nissan Dovid Dubov,
   chabad.org
5. The Transmission of Kabbalah by
   Aryeh Kaplan
6. 18 Facts About Rabbi Nachman of
   Breslov by Menachem Posner
7. Likutei Moharan, Tinyana 25
8. Ibid, Tinyana 2
9. Chayei Moharan 404
10. Kokhvei Ohr, Anshei Moharan, 4
    [Jerusalem 1983 ed.] p. 69
11. The Rebbe's Rosh Hashanah by Rabbi
    Dovid Sears, breslev.com
12. Tzaddik #367
13. breslovcenter.blogspot.com/2012/12/
    reb-nosons-yahrtzeit.html
14. Reb Noson by breslov.org
15. The Rebbe: A Brief Biography,
    chabad.org
16. "Conversation with Martin Luther
    King," 2
17. jewishvirtuallibrary.org/
    abraham-joshua-heschel
18. "Conversation with Martin Luther
    King," 2
19. kinginstitute.stanford.
    edu/encyclopedia/
    heschel-abraham-joshua
20. Wikipedia and happyminyan.org/
    Rabbi-shlomo-carlebach
21. Wikipedia
22. everything.explained.today/
    Aryeh_Kaplan
23. Biography of Rabbi Lord Jonathan
    Sacks, Rabbisacks.org
24. genesisprize.org/lifetime-
    achievement-award/2021/biography
25. Ibid
26. Biography of Rabbi Lord Jonathan
    Sacks, Rabbisacks.org

Glossary

Ahava: love אהבה

Aliyah: ascent עליה

Avot: Patriarchs אבות

B'nei Yisrael: Children of Israel בני ישראל

Baal Teshuvah: "A returnee", one who has become observant of the commandments בעל תשובה

Beit HaMikdash: Holy Temple בית המקדש

Bitachon: trust ביטחון

Brachot: blessings ברכות

Breslov: ברסלב is a branch of chassidism founded by Rebbe Nachman of Breslov (1772–1810)

ChaBaD: חב"ד is an acronym for *Chochmah, Binah, Daat* which is also popularized as the name of the worldwide chassidic movement

Chazal: our Sages חז"ל

Chiyut: life חיות

Da'at: higher perception דעת

Dibur: speech דיבור

Echad: One

Ein Sof: אין סוף literally means 'without end' and is used to refer to Hashem, the Infinite, as enclothed in Creation

Emunah: faith אמונה

Esav: Esau עשו

Dveykut: clinging, attaching oneself to God דבקות

Gematria: numerical value of a Hebrew word גמטריא

Hashem: י-ה-ו-ה / השם literally means 'The Name' and is a euphemism for the Tetragrammaton (Yud-Kay-Vav-Kay), which is never spoken, as it appears in the Torah.

Hashgachah Pratit: Divine Providence השגחה פרטית

Kabbalah: קבלה literally means 'received' and is a term used to refer to the mystical tradition of the Torah.

Kadosh: holy קדוש

Kavanah: sincerity or intention כוונה

Kelipah: קליפה means 'peel' or 'shell' and is used by Kabbalists to describe coverings of impurity which conceal holiness.

Kohelet: The book of Ecclesiastes קהלת

Kohen Gadol: High Priest כהן גדול

Kulo Shabbat: entirely Shabbat כולו שבת

Mashiach (the Messiah): literally means the anointed one משיח

Mekudash: sanctified מקודש

Midbar: desert מדבר

Midrash: מדרש is a term that refers to the anthology of rabbinic scriptural commentary.

Mikdash: Holy Temple מקדש

Mikvah: is a ritual bath used for spiritual purification מקוה

Mishkan: Tabernacle, is a portable sanctuary משכן

Mishlei: Proverbs משלי

Mitzvah/Mitzvot: Commandments מצוה/מצוות

Moshe: Moses משה

Na'aseh v'Nishma: "We will do and we will hear" נעשה ונשמע

Nevuah: prophecy נבואה

Olam: world (also 'concealment') עולם

Olam Haba: the World to Come עולם הבא

Or: Light אור

Or Ein Sof: Light of the Infinite אור אין סוף

Parashah: portion of the Torah פרשה

Pasuk: verse פסוק

Ruach HaKodesh: the spirit of prophecy רוח הקודש

Safek: doubt ספק

Sefirah: ספירה (plural. Sefirot / ספירות) a channel of Divine energy or attribute used in creation

Shabbat: Sabbath שבת

Shechinah: Divine Presence שכינה

Simchah: joy שמחה

Sitra Achra: the other side, the side of creation that opposes holiness סטרא אחרא

Tahor: pure or spiritually fit טהור

Talmud: תלמוד is the Mishnah and the Gemara, a collection of writings that covers the full gamut of Jewish law and tradition, compiled and edited between the third and sixth centuries.

Tefillah: prayer תפילה

Tehillim: Psalms תהילים

Teshuvah: Repentance (literally means "returning") תשובה

Tomeh: impure or spiritually unfit טמא

Tzedakah: charity צדקה

Tzimtzum: the contraction of God's infinity into our finitude צמצום

Yaakov: Jacob יעקב

Yeridah: descent ירידה

Yetzer Hara: evil inclination יצר הרע

Yetzer HaTov: good inclination יצר הטוב

Yitzchak: Isaac יצחק

Some of these terms and concepts are expounded in the 'Key Kabbalistic Concepts' chapter.

Gematria—Hebrew Letter Numerology

LETTER	VALUE	LETTER	VALUE
Aleph א	1	Lamed ל	30
Bet ב	2	Mem מ	40
Gimel ג	3	Nun נ	50
Dalet ד	4	Samech ס	60
Hei ה	5	Ayin ע	70
Vav ו	6	Peh פ	80
Zayin ז	7	Tsadi צ	90
Chet ח	8	Kuf ק	100
Tet ט	9	Resh ר	200
Yud י	10	Shin ש	300
Kaf כ	20	Tav ת	400

Alternate values for the five end-letters, MaNzPaKh

500	Kaf (final)	ך
600	Mem (final)	ם
700	Nun (final)	ן
800	Peh (final)	ף
900	Tzadi (final)	ץ

The Order of the Ten Sefirot

כתר	*(Keter)*	Crown
חכמה	*(Chochmah)*	Wisdom
בינה	*(Binah)*	Understanding
[דעת	*(Daat)*	Knowledge
חסד	*(Chesed)*	Loving-Kindness
גבורה	*(Gevurah)*	Strength
תפארת	*(Tiferet)*	Beauty
נצח	*(Netzach)*	Victory
הוד	*(Hod)*	Empathy
יסוד	*(Yesod)*	Foundation
מלכות	*(Malchut)*	Sovereignty

The Sefirot in Relation to the Body

כתר	*(Keter)*	Skull
חכמה	*(Chochmah)*	Right brain
בינה	*(Binah)*	Left brain
[דעת	*(Daat)*	Middle brain
חסד	*(Chesed)*	Right arm
גבורה	*(Gevurah)*	Left arm
תפארת	*(Tiferet)*	Torso
נצח	*(Netzach)*	Right leg
הוד	*(Hod)*	Left leg
יסוד	*(Yesod)*	Sexual organ *(brit)*
מלכות	*(Malchut)*	Feet

Alternatively: *Chochmah* corresponds to the brain/mind, *Binah* to the heart.

Alternatively: *Malchut* corresponds to woman, or the mouth.

**   To dive deeper into the Ten Sefirot, the five levels of the soul, and the mystical connection between each aspect of the human body, I suggest reading *Anatomy of the Soul* by Chaim Kramer.

The Seven Supernal Shepherds

Avraham	Chesed (Loving-Kindness)
Yitzchak	Gevurah (Strength, Restraint)
Yaakov	Tiferet (Harmony, Beauty, Truth)
Moshe	Netzach (Victory, Endurance)
Aharon	Hod (Splendor)
Yosef	Yesod (Foundation)
David	Malchut (Kingship)

the other side

back to its source

the world
is full
of enough
dissonance

produce
melody
perform
alchemy

sift the good notes
from the bad
the serene
from the siren song

step in rhythm
grow in concert

we are all notes
in this
divine
orchestra
of existence

When everything is running smoothly, it's easy to feel faithful—everything seems aligned. But in those times, too, we sometimes think foolishly that it is because of our own doing and not that of Hashem. In those times, we can get shaken up and fall from on high back to a space of humility, back to a space of questioning. This is all so that we can eventually remember that it is all in the hands of Hashem, and that all that we have has to be connected back to Hashem, that we are meant to spiritualize reality, not materialize it, and that is done via *teshuva*, meaning "to return" to Hashem.

The magic of Hashem and the magic in us is concealed; making every ascent feel that much more sublime because it isn't a straight line to be taken for granted. The ascent comes from the descent; perpetually inspired by clouded clarity that permeates our universe. The magic of it isn't an illusion; it's the moments that we don't see the magic that are.

Torah, Kabbalah and Chassidut are composed of the Hebrew letters that continuously breathe life into materiality. These letters are beyond poems from the Infinite One, brought down as ineffable revelations. They are the building blocks that parallel Yakov's ladder, upon which the angels perpetually ascend and descend. This parallels our own struggle and redemption in the antechamber of this world — a transient path towards the banquet hall. The final revelation and redemption will consist of the refinement that each of us has manifested, elevating physicality towards its spiritual source, the Infinite One. Because there is nothing but Hashem save for our frequent and temporal inabilities to see the hidden truth all around us.

Made in the USA
Las Vegas, NV
08 February 2023

67143604R00129